Praise for *Virtuous L*

I0037171

""Ethical leadership has never been more important than today! *Virtuous Leadership* is the perfect guide to understanding the blend of character, values, and behaviors every leader needs at their foundation. A must read!"--**Dr. Marshall Goldsmith**, the *Thinkers50* #1 Executive Coach and New York Times bestselling author of *The Earned Life, Triggers*, and *What Got You Here Won't Get You There.*

"On a daily basis we hear of and read about unethical and amoral leaders in our institutions and business organizations. Poll after poll show that people have lost confidence and trust in our leaders as a result. This calls into question the validity of leader selection and development. Ray Williams' new book, *Virtuous Leadership* presents a timely and compelling argument for a focus on virtues and good character. Presenting both a philosophical and practical analysis, backed by research, of a rationale for this focus, he also provides practical suggestions on emphasizing good character and virtues in leadership selection, promotion and training. *Virtuous Leadership* is an important book that can be a valuable reference for institutions and organizations in their efforts to bring back credibility and respect for our leaders."-- **Emma Seppälä, Ph.D.,** Science Director, Stanford University Center For Compassion And Altruism Research And Education and Co-Director Wellness, Yale Center for Emotional Intelligence.

"So glad to see an author and thought leader such as Ray Williams tackle one of the thorniest issues facing our society today — incivility. In *Virtuous Leadership,* Williams explores the breakdown of cultural norms and the false sense of permissiveness that makes individuals feel they can be openly hostile to others. Fortunately Williams provides remedies for this dilemma — leadership rooted in strong character. The book discusses the virtues of humility and vulnerability as well as the need for resilience and courage in the face of adversity. *Virtuous Leadership* is a welcome addition any leader's bookshelf." —**John Baldoni,** 2021 IFLD Hall of Fame Mentor; 2022 Global Gurus Top 20; Inc.com Top 50 Leadership Expert; Inc.com Top 100 Leadership Speaker; Author of 15 books published in 10 languages; Master Corporate Executive Coach; Member of Marshall Goldsmith 100 Coaches.

"Ray Williams' new book, *Virtuous Leadership* is timely and important. On a daily basis stories of unethical, and amoral leaders of low character have eroded people's confidence in political and business leaders. Traditional approaches to selecting and training leaders have focused too much on the mechanics of leading. Williams argues persuasively that it's time to return to a focus on good character and virtuous leadership to restore our confidence in leaders, and he makes practical suggestions on leadership development to achieve this. *The Virtuous Leader* is a book that every leader should read and keep on the shelf." —**Professor M.S. Rao, Ph.D.** He was ranked #1 Thought Leader and Influencer in HR globally by Thinkers360; the Father of "Soft Leadership", Keynote Speaker & Author of Over 50 Leadership Books

"In bookstores and libraries you will find numerous books on leadership style, leadership competencies, but very few that focus on leadership character and virtues. Perhaps it's because good character seems like an old fashioned idea. Yet character is such a central, important element of leadership. In many ways character defines how we engage the world around us. It reflects our values, our behaviors, and attitudes.

Ray Williams' new book, *Virtuous Leadership* is both a sobering and optimistic look at the state of leadership in our organizations. The current trend referred to as "The Great Resignation" or "Great Reset" refers to the reluctance of workers returning to work after the COVID pandemic abatement because they no longer wish to work in organizations with toxic leaders and in toxic work environments.

Williams describes how the general public and employees have lost confidence and trust in leaders of our organizations as a result of unethical and corrupt behaviors, and argues convincingly for a return to the basics of good character and virtuous behavior to restore that confidence and trust. He also shows how leadership development initiatives based on character development and virtues can be a bedrock for selecting and developing great leaders.

Virtuous Leadership is an insightful book worthy of a thoughtful read. Williams makes a compelling argument that people today are looking for role models who not only exhibit the skills required for effective leadership, but also display integrity, courage, compassion, and humanity. A return to good character and virtues can be the path to do just that."—**Dan Pontefract,** Founder, Pontefract Group; keynote speaker; leadership strategist and author of four best-selling books, including the award-winning *Lead. Care. Win.*

 Leaders are judged by how effectively they achieve their organization's goals and manage themselves and others in the organization. A critical part of a leaders' success reflects the degree to which they are seen as possessing the highest of integrity and ethical conduct. Ray Williams' new book, *Virtuous Leadership* insightfully describes and advocates an important focus on virtuous behavior by leaders of good character. It's a must read by leaders and organization owners.--**Bing Chen,** President & CEO Atlas Corp. (Seaspan Corporation and APR Energy Limited)

"In the fast-paced entrepreneurial world, proper leadership can be forgotten. *Virtuous Leadership* is a must read for any leader and founder looking to develop today's solid organization with leadership built on appropriate and timeless character traits, values and compassion for a bright tomorrow for all."-- **Stephanie Frank,** Co-Founder, The Holisec Group (creator of TheGoodLife.ai), 4x Int'l Best Selling Author, *The Accidental Millionaire.*

Virtuous Leadership

The Character Secrets of Great Leaders

Ray Williams

Copyright @ 2022 Ray Williams

All rights reserved.

No part of this publication may be reproduced, distributed, or transmitted in any form or by any means, including photocopying, recording, or other electronic or mechanical methods, without the prior written permission of the author, except in the case of brief cited quotations embodied in critical reviews and certain other non-commercial uses permitted by copyright law.

Includes bibliographical references.

ISBN: 978-1-7348979-8-2

Dedication

This book is dedicated to my father Brinley Williams, who was a father, husband, friend and leader of consummate good character, who exhibited the best of virtuous and ethical behavior throughout a challenging and traumatic lifetime, and who always encouraged me to do the right thing.

CONTENTS

Acknowledgements

I am fortunate to have had such highly respected and generous people help me in the completion of this book. My sincere gratitude is extended to Marshall Goldsmith, Emma Seppälä, Ph.D., John Baldoni, Professor M.S. Rao, Ph.D, Dan Pontefract, Bing Chen and Stephanie Frank for their kind endorsements of my book.

My thanks are extended to Stephanie Frank, for her insightful review and editing of my book.

And finally, I am forever grateful to my wife, partner and friend, Diane Williams, who generously gave her time and talents in editing my manuscript and for her never-ending inspiration, love and support.

Preface

"Ninety-nine percent of leadership failures are failures of character."

—General Norman Schwarzkopf

Although they may leave a lasting impression on the world, autocratic, toxic and destructive leaders are rarely held in high regard. Great leaders win the respect and admiration of their followers based on their good character. People today want to follow leaders who not only exhibit the necessary leadership competencies, but also leaders who exhibit qualities and virtues of good character, such as integrity, emotional intelligence, compassion and service.

My previous books, *Toxic Bosses: Practical Wisdom for Developing Wise, Ethical and Moral Leaders; Macho Men: How Toxic Masculinity Harms Us All and What To Do About It; I Know Myself and Neither Do You; and Eye of the Storm: How Mindful Leaders Can Transform Chaotic Workplaces* examined both the dark and light sides of leadership in organizations.

Virtuous Leadership: The Character Secrets of Great Leaders, is the last book in this series and examines in dept how the qualities of good character and virtuous behavior should be the cornerstone of good leadership, with suggestions on leadership development initiatives that will build on that cornerstone.

Virtues, ethics, good character and morality are cited as being crucial to good leadership in numerous theories of leadership. Yet there has been insufficient attention to understanding how to develop or embed these virtues and notions of good character in practice.

In bookstores and libraries you will find numerous books on leadership style, and leadership competencies, but very few that focus on leadership character. For some reason we have lost sight of character and virtuous behavior. One reason may be that our education system and organizations have focused on practical competencies. Or perhaps it's because good character seems like an old fashioned idea. Or that focusing on ethical and virtuous behavior is much more difficult to do than focusing on concrete procedures, execution and technical expertise. Or perhaps it's because designing and implementing a leadership development program based on virtues and good character is more difficult than current typical programs.

Yet character is such a central, important element of leadership. In many ways character defines how we engage the world around us. It reflects our values, our behaviors, and attitudes.

The current trend referred to as "The Great Resignation" or "Great Reset" refers to the reluctance of workers returning to work after the COVID pandemic abatement because they no longer wish to work in organizations with toxic leaders and in toxic work environments. They look to organizational cultures that value workers well-being, mental health and personal fulfillment. And it's clear that few leadership development programs address these needs and a structure that focuses on leaders' good character and virtuous behaviors.

My consulting and coaching firm has delivered leader training and coaching to hundreds executives and their associates for over 30 years. With this experience, I discovered a few truths:

- People who choose to rise to the challenge of leadership desire to be virtuous leaders and are hungry to be taught how to be of good character in a culture they can be proud of.
- People desire to work for leaders whose virtues are modeled in their daily behavior.
- There is an understandable level of new generational cynicism developed as a result of well-publicized ethical lapses of self-centered short-term management, be it business or government.
- Far too often, executives are recruited and promoted based on what I would call an external demonstration of ability — financial success for shareholders, organizational strategies and plans with little or no consideration for the character, ethics and virtues of leaders.

In the book I use the term morality, ethics, virtues and character. While they are not the same, they do overlap.

Morality can be defined as a set of standards that enable people to live cooperatively in groups in a way that is "right" and "acceptable." Sometimes, acting in a moral manner means individuals must sacrifice their own short-term interests to benefit society. Individuals who go against these standards may be considered immoral. Morality isn't fixed. What's considered acceptable in one culture might not be acceptable in another culture although some morals such as honesty seem to transcend across the globe and across time. Researchers have discovered that these morals are somewhat universal: courage, fairness, cooperation, love, and respect.

Ethics refers to a community or organization's moral values, principles or rules as opposed to personal values. As such, it is concerned with rights and responsibilities and how moral decisions are made.

Virtues can be defined as moral excellence, goodness, admirable qualities or traits. They are universal and recognized by all cultures as basic qualities of well-being.

Character can be defined as a combination of mental characteristics and behaviors that distinguishes a person. In the context of this book, character refers to good character, which reflects moral strength and ethical qualities, and reflects a number of virtues.

In this book, I make reference to two leaders with whom I was engaged as their executive coach. My approach to coaching leaders has always had a focus on leadership character, and the two individuals exhibited vastly different characters and behaviors, which had a direct connection to their success in their organizations.

Much of leadership in the past can be described as "reorganizing the deck chairs on the Titanic." It focused a great deal on the minute detail of how an organization ran while it was steaming ahead into chaos. Despite the expectations of the general public that leaders act in a moral, virtuous and ethical manner, and demonstrate good character, we've seen the opposite at great cost to people and institutions.

While it may seem like a simplistic argument for returning to focus on the values and behaviors of leaders that amount to "doing the right thing," doing no harm, and serving people and society, I believe those ancient philosophical beliefs are worth embracing again.

Each chapter of the book examines in detail the various elements of good character and virtuous leadership as well as some practical suggestions for robust leadership development strategies for organizations. At the end of each chapter there is also questions to consider as a follow-up.

It is my hope that this book provides a cogent argument for reevaluating the current state of leadership in organizations and institutions and an impetus for recruiting and promoting virtuous leaders of good character.

Introduction

Why We Need Virtuous Leaders of Good Character

"To dissolve the unholy alliance between corrupt business and corrupt politics, is the first task of the statesmanship of the day."

— President Theodore Roosevelt

The lack of moral behavior and good character are major themes in research on leadership failures.

The crisis and tragedy playing out in Ukraine are a reflection of Vladimir Putin and his government's lack of moral fiber and virtue. The worst in leadership is demonstrated by the Russian attack, which has killed and injured innocent civilians.

The deceit and dishonesty of the Bush administration during the invasion of Iraq, the corrupt actions of the Trump administration regarding the 2020 Presidential election, and the financial crisis of 2008–2009, all serve as examples of the urgent need for morally upright leaders in the United States.

Large egos, a lack of humility, and ignorance of potential harm done to others or the cultures in which they functioned are signs of a person's lack of moral character and virtue. In essence, all of these actions and behaviors were character flaws.

This "dirty hands problem" has affected the performance of CEOs at major firms like Enron, Volkswagen, Wells Fargo, Theranos, WorldCom,

Global Crossing, Anderson Consulting, and Tyco. These businesses, along with others, were all susceptible to the leaders' avarice in various ways, from fraud to fabricating or obscuring financial data. These instances of dishonest leadership are caused in part by the character crises of the particular leaders. As a result, workers have lost their jobs, businesses have gone bankrupt, employee retirement plans have been eliminated, cynicism and distrust have increased, and the general public is mistrusting.

According to the Securities and Exchange Commission, Ernst & Young cheated on the ethical portion of the Certified Public Accountant test and suppressed proof of the activity from regulators. The SEC said that it has penalized Ernst & Young $100 million, the highest amount ever imposed on an accounting company. In addition to breaching accounting regulations, the corporation "hindered" the investigation into the wrongdoing by concealing information from the SEC, according to the regulator.

In 2019, the SEC penalized KPMG, another of the "big four" accounting firms, $50 million for falsifying internal training exams and altering earlier audit work after receiving stolen data from a sector watchdog organization.

According to a global report published by Transparency International, corruption is a serious issue around the world, and studies have revealed that the US rates poorly when compared to other Western nations. Some analysts contend that the US slide is caused by dwindling confidence in democratic institutions and, more lately, by poor oversight of the financial system related to the pandemic under the Trump administration. In the annual *Corruption Perceptions Index (CPI)*, the United States dropped from a high of 76 in 2015 to a low of 67 out of a possible score of 100, far below other Western nations.

A major factor in the United States' decreasing ranking, according to Scott Greytak, the advocacy director for Transparency International's U.S. office, is what he calls a "decay" in its democratic institutions. Gretyak made the important claim that politics, the media, and organizations today appeared to be fertile with misinformation, fake news, and record-setting amounts of untraceable money in the 2020 elections, which contributed to the public's lack of faith in American elections.

Greytak cited a joint investigation by *BuzzFeed News* and the International Consortium of Investigative Journalists from last year that revealed "how major banks had knowingly allowed trillions of dollars of suspect financial transactions to go ahead, enabling drug kingpins, kleptocrats, and terrorists," as examples of the "series of really bombshell exposés by media outlets that are demonstrating how much dirty money is flowing into the United States' financial system."

The Payment Protection Program loans, which were supposed to support small businesses during the COVID pandemic but instead went to large corporations like defense contractors, the international fast food chain Shake Shack, and the Los Angeles Lakers. And the Trump administration funneled millions of dollars in coronavirus aid to companies with potential conflicts of interests, including some owned by Jared Kushner's family and others housed in buildings operated by the president's real estate company, according to records made public.

Jim Kouzes and Barry Z. Posner published an article in *Leadership Excellence* which states "But somewhere along the way to the New Millennium notions of ethics, morality, honesty, character and personal discipline came to be viewed as quaint — at least by those from the me-first, free agent school of corporate strategy. People got sucked into the idea that leadership was all about extrinsic rewards, and they started offering very creative ways to attract talent to the good life. The intrinsic reasons for doing something important —really caring about the people and the purpose — too often got lost in the hyperbole."

They go on to say this about leadership: "Leaders are judged by how they spend their time, how they react to critical incidents, the stories they tell, the questions they ask, the language and symbols they choose, and the measures they use. Nothing fuels the fires of cynicism more than hypocrisy, and leaders will need to be constantly vigilant about aligning what they practice with what they preach. If you dream of leaving a legacy then you'd better heed the Golden Rule of Leadership: DWYSYWD: Do What You Say You Will Do."

Corruption and Ethical Leadership Behavior are Mutually Exclusive

Toxic Bosses: Practical Wisdom for Developing Wise, Ethical, and Moral Leaders is the title of my book in which I argue: "Research has indicated that for many years, the company's subpar financial performance was the primary factor in chief executives being fired. The year 2018 saw a shift in that. According to the survey, 39% of the 89 CEOs who left their positions in 2018 did so because of unethical activity that was connected to fraud, bribery, or insider trading, among other ethical transgressions."

24

I also reference Stephen Chen's research, which was published in the *Journal of Business Ethics,* which states that "misreporting performance improves the CEO's confidence, which in turn raises the urge to misreport performance to feed an ever-increasing ego. Statements from independent financial analysts and the media that applaud their initiatives can encourage this expansion. And they are not only limited to financial information."

Chen continues: "These ethical challenges include deceptive advertising, advertising to children, and the exploitation of women. Current techniques of analyzing commercials may not be adequate for some of today's contentious or innovative campaigns, as evidenced by the fact that potentially unethical advertisements are reaching the market."

According to financial analyst Steven Pearlstein, who wrote in *The Washington Post,* "maximizing shareholder value has meant doing whatever is necessary to boost the share price this quarter and the next. This practice is inculcated in many business schools, enforced by corporate lawyers, and demanded by activist investors and Wall Street analysts. Over the years, a sole focus on shareholder profit has been cited as justification for taking advantage of or cheating on customers, underpaying employees and suppliers, evading taxes, and lavishing executives with stock options. This false and perverted idea that business just exists for financial gain for the shareholders (and greedy CEOs) lies at the basis of much of what many find so repulsive about American capitalism, including the ruthlessness, greed, and unfairness."

The U.S. Ethics and Compliance Initiative (ECI), the first non-profit organization in the ethics and compliance field, is also a membership and research organization made up of organizations from all industries, each committed to advancing the highest standards of integrity in their business practices. The ECI has reported on the existence of unethical practices in American organizations, presenting some shocking facts.

The culture of the company, according to ECI, is the one factor that has the most impact on employee behavior. Wrongdoing is drastically decreased in organizations and societies with strong ethical norms. However, according to ECI's assessment of American businesses, only one in five employees say their workplace has such a culture. Over the previous ten years, this situation has remained substantially constant. Furthermore, a pattern that hasn't much changed since 2000 is that 40% of employees in 2018 thought that their firm had a bad ethical culture.

"Is America Turning Into a Banana Republic?" is the question posed by Robin Wright in an article in *The New Yorker*. According to her, "the main tenet of 'banana-ism' is that of 'kleptocracy,' where people in positions of power use their time in office to maximize their personal earnings, always making sure that any shortfall is made up by those unfortunates whose everyday life entails earning money rather than producing it." She comes to the conclusion that the United States satisfies those criteria.

Unethical Conduct Is Contagious in the Workplace

The Ethics Resource Center (ERC), an independent research firm for the advancement of high ethical standards and practices in public and private organizations, conducted the National Business Ethics Survey of almost 4,700 employees. The results show that the percentage of companies with a weak ethical culture is increasing, as is the number of employees who experienced retaliation for reporting observed misconduct. According to the report's conclusion, "American business may be on the verge of a significant downward change in ethical behavior."

The following were some of the other findings of the ERC report: The five most frequent observed misbehavior occurrences were misusing company time (33%), followed by abusive behavior (21%), misusing company resources (20%), lying to employees (20%), and violating corporate Internet use restrictions (20%). As predicted, a high ethical culture and less witnessed wrongdoing have a very substantial association. Only 29% of businesses with a strong ethical culture reported misconduct, compared to 90% of businesses with a weak ethical culture, according to the ERC report.

In his book, *Leadership From The Inside Out,* Kevin Cashman claims that leaders whose focus is primarily external and focused on control, fear, self-interest, and winning at all costs, have contributed to bad leadership. This leadership crisis may be attributed to leaders choosing to operate out of this mindset. According to Cashman, people should act in ways that aren't typical of them (which he calls leading from the inside-out). This enables a leader to be inspired by truth, goal, transparency, trust, and compassion. The attitude of the day, which is centered on financial gain and a consumer mentality, further exacerbates this issue. Leaders are pursuing performance targets due to this consumer drive, forgetting that lasting beneficial effect is based on the "kind of people they are and not only on power, titles, and positions."

In the book *Intrinsic CSR and Competition*, edited by W. Wehrmeyer et al., Mathias Schüz of the School of Management and Law at Zurich University claimed that "there is a comprehensible cause-effect loop between the virtuous behavior of a company, its trustworthy reputation, and appeal to stakeholders."

According to Schüz, the absence of ethical awareness among senior managers is a common occurrence in business. He claims that ethical leadership is frequently requested but infrequently provided.

According to Schüz, investing in training programs to foster moral behavior will pay dividends for both individuals and companies. "Integrity" is a virtue that allows one to act morally upright in a given circumstance while keeping in mind their own capabilities. According to Schüz, moral behavior promotes self-responsibility and excellent character rather than relying solely on a compliance-based ethics of responsibilities. Hundreds of laws and tight compliance processes, he contends, only serve to increase distrust and denunciation. They ought to be diminished, and integrity-boosting initiatives ought to be added.

The Role of Business Schools

Professor Sumantra Ghoshal submitted an article for publication in the journal *Academy of Management Learning and Education* just before he passed away at the age of 55. The piece contains harsh criticism of business education initiatives.

It was included in the magazine together with a piece by Stanford University's Jeffrey Pfeffer, a leading management researcher in the US and one of the publication's most vehement critics of business schools.

Business schools merely need to avoid doing a lot of the things they already do, according to Ghoshal: "Business schools do not need to do a great deal more to help prevent future Enrons," he wrote, "Many of the greatest excesses of contemporary management techniques have their origins in a collection of notions that have arisen from business school academics over the previous thirty years."

Business schools are specifically targeted for criticism by Ghoshal due to the "dehumanizing influence of contemporary economics on management thought."

In response to his article, "Bad Management Theories Are Destroying Good Management Practices," Pfeffer, Rosabeth Moss Kanter of Harvard Business School, Donald Hambrick of Penn State University, John Gapper of the *Financial Times*, Lex Donaldson of the Australian Graduate School of Management, and Henry Mintzberg of McGill University are among the top management theorists who provided comments.

Pfeffer strongly concurs with Ghoshal's criticism of economics: if anything, Pfeffer claims, "he [Ghoshal] understates the potential negative consequences of the expanding dominance of economics over the social sciences." As it has done with political science and law, Pfeffer says, as it is doing with sociology and psychology, economics is undoubtedly displacing management and organizational science.

In order for shareholders to benefit from limited liability, Ghoshal contends that they "do not own the company - not in the sense that they own their homes or their automobiles." Additionally, he claims that "the majority of stockholders can sell their stocks much more easily than the majority of employees can find another job." Employees of a corporation incur more risks than stockholders do in every meaningful sense.

The majority of well-known management theories place little emphasis on the social and moral principles necessary for effective administration, instead favoring considerations of self-interest and opportunism. The façade of knowledge, in Ghoshal's words, "has caused us to increasingly focus on the negative problem as a result of which we have made little analytical progress on the positive problem in the previous thirty years, at enormous expense to our students, to companies, and to society."

Ghoshal and Pfeffer contend that business schools should place greater emphasis on "the wisdom of common sense" rather than on mathematical models that are friendly to science.

Economics is a "neat and tidy" field, Rosabeth Moss Kanter of the Harvard Business School adds, "People are messy. The theories Ghoshal criticizes have a scientific, analytical, and statistical bent that makes them appear difficult, but in reality, in practice, the so-called soft concepts, which hold that management is an art involving people, are much tougher. Executives state that. MBAs from Harvard Business School concur. And after five years, they frequently regret not enrolling in more people-focused courses instead of finance courses."

Pfeffer and Ghoshal present a substantial body of data that indicates that studying business and economics is linked to moral and social flaws. Evidence of that was published by Donald McCabe who conducted a study of 16,000 undergraduate students at 31 schools and universities, and the results showed that business students committed nearly twice as many cheating offences as the average student.

Pfeffer, Fabrizio Ferraro and Robert I. Sutton cite data in an article in the *Academy of Management Review* that demonstrates students who major in economics are more likely to betray coworkers, act selfishly, and have a stronger predisposition to corruption.

According to Pfeffer, management education needs to become more professional, just like the medical and legal professions. "Ethics and morals are very much a part of medical school or law school, but they tend to fall by the wayside in business schools," the Pfeffer claims. Although it is unclear whether this will become a widespread trend, some business schools have started to take action.

According to Kanter, "a growing amount of scholarly research demonstrates the link between profitability and considerate treatment of employees and customers, or between sustained financial success and a focus on all stakeholders... Maybe the right theories will win out in the end. If the world requires them, they will."

Final Thoughts

Corruption, unethical and amoral behavior of leaders and their organizations has existed throughout human history the world over. And there have been efforts by international organizations such as the

United Nations, The International Monetary Fund and public watchdog organizations to raise awareness and press for laws and regulations to curtail the problems.

Yet they persist.

I've chosen to focus on the United States because it has such an important impact globally. The problem is particularly concerning today due to the signs of a divided nation in terms of both values and politics. An increasing number of experts are warning that the continued escalation of unethical and amoral behavior of leaders can be a powerful force that is threatening American democracy itself.

Final Thoughts and Questions to Consider

An ever increasing number of experts are sounding the warning bells about unethical practices in government and business, along with the prevalence of corrupt and amoral leaders.

Here are Some Questions Worth Considering

1. Are the problems described in this chapter just reflective of similar problems in the past? Or are we seeing an escalation in severity?

2. Why do we continue to choose the kind of leader with traits such as narcissism, psychopathy and greed when we know that we would be better served with leaders who are humble, and servant leaders of high moral character? What needs to change?

Chapter 1

Understanding What is Good Character

"Good character is not formed in a week or a month. It is created little by little, day by day. Protracted and patient effort is needed to develop good character."

— Heraclitus

Character is defined by the dictionary as a person's overall characteristics. We all have personalities, some good, some bad, and occasionally both depending on the circumstance.

It usually means that a person is a nice person deserving of trust, respect, and admiration when we say they have good character. However, they might not be faultless.

Therefore, when we say that a person has good character, we mean that their nature is defined by admirable attributes like honesty, courage, and compassion. Even when their activities might be risky or harmful to their well-being, people with good character typically follow moral values as their guide. In other words, they act morally even if it costs them.

Ethics and morality are demonstrated through good character. Stephen Covey, a management guru, asserts that "Our character is essentially a composite of our habits. They consistently and daily express our character since they are reliable, frequently unconscious routines."

People can be of either good or horrifically bad character. Leaders like Hitler, Stalin, or Putin, for instance, would be viewed as having a dark or evil characters. And the virtues exhibited by leaders like Mandela, Gandhi, or Martin Luther King are viewed as having good character.

Modern Interpretations of Character and Virtue in Leadership

There are many different ways to define good character, including "doing the right thing even when you don't think anyone is looking, [or even if they are]" and "a persistent reputation of personal honesty, trustworthiness, virtuousness, and integrity."

Character is a collection of nurtured, admirable qualities that, when they become habits, define a person as a whole and make the person exemplary.

A focus is placed on character traits, values, and virtues while evaluating a person's character.

Habitual patterns of thought, behavior, and emotion that are regarded to be largely consistent in individuals across settings and throughout time is how traits are described. There are no set traits. Extroverts can learn to regulate and temper their extroverted tendencies when necessary, whereas introverts may be able to learn how to act in a less introverted manner.

In the psychological literature, a huge variety of personality traits have been discussed. However, five major personality domains or dimensions have emerged as a result of statistical methods like factor analysis, and they are now frequently employed in a variety of ways for hiring and evaluating employees.

The "Big Five" traits are:

- Conscientiousness

- Openness to experience

- Extroversion

- Agreeableness

- Neuroticism

Some personality traits can be inherited, according to research. For example, according to certain studies, identical twins have more features in common than non-identical twins, for instance. Through events in life and the influence of others, traits can also change, become stronger, or become weaker.

Values are opinions or beliefs about what is significant or deserving in the eyes of a person. Values affect how we act. Our values and the extent to which we apply them to decisions and actions might change over the course of our life.

The societies and communities in which a person lives have an impact on their values. The right to freedom and the pursuit of happiness are highly cherished in Western democracies. Order, tranquilly, nonviolence, and equality are valued in other cultures. Some of us develop values based on the teachings of those religions.

Ethics and moral principles like honesty, integrity, compassion, justice, generosity, and social responsibility can also be used to describe values. These moral principles may be held with strength or weakness, and they affect behavior appropriately.

People may profess values, but when their actions don't match those values, dissonance results. Most people encounter value conflicts throughout their lives when forced to choose between potentially incompatible values. People become conflicted and may not uphold their principles, for instance, when loyalty conflicts with honesty, justice conflicts with pragmatism, or social responsibility conflicts with a duty to shareholders. They also feel guilty, angry, and embarrassed when their acts don't align with their ideals. By explaining or outright rejecting their behavior, downplaying the consequences, or blaming others, people attempt to reduce such cognitive dissonance.

Virtues are actions that are usually seen as being indicative of excellent character, such as kindness and temperance. A couple of the virtues are reflected in personality qualities that are generally stable dispositional factors, such conscientiousness and openness to new things. If not overwhelmed by other pressures and influences like rewards or peer pressure, certain personality qualities predispose people to act in specific morally upright ways.

Origins of Virtue in History and Culture

The Golden Rule, or the Christian maxim of "do unto others as you would have them do unto you," is well-known to most of us and is echoed in various religions. For instance, the precept of Buddhism states:

"Do not harm others in ways that you would harm yourself." According to Hinduism, one should "not do to others what would bring anguish if done to oneself."

According to Confucianism, one should "do unto others as one would have them do unto you;" according to Islam, "No one [really] believes] until he wishes for his brother what he desires for himself;" according to Judaism, "What you despise, do not do to anyone;" "Consider your neighbor's success as your success, and consider your neighbor's failure as your failure," according to Taoist philosophy. There is an implied appreciation for human respect throughout these various faiths despite these variations in form (i.e., "do unto others" versus "do not do").

The Greeks believed that character was a defining characteristic of a person's beliefs and actions as measured in terms of values and strength of will in the early 5th century BC. There are two types of human excellences, according to the great Greek philosopher Aristotle: excellences of mind and excellences of character. Excellences of character, or *ethikai aretai* in Greek, are typically translated as "moral excellences" or "moral virtues." The adjective *ethikos,* which means "ethical," is a cognate of the noun ethos, which means "character." According to Aristotle, having excellent character means acting morally both toward others and toward oneself. For Aristotle, moral virtues include both internal (like restraint and moderation) and outward (like charity) virtues (such as generosity and compassion).

Being able to regulate or control our emotional responses is essential for the growth of moral character, according to both Aristotle and Plato.

According to Aristotle, virtue is what makes a person good. He held that the non-stereotypical self-love that distinguishes the virtuous person comes from friendships where people grow to value the well-being of others over their own interests.

In the past, philosophers believed that developing one's character was the responsibility of the person and that qualities were learned via trial and error through "some activity of the soul." According to the *Doctrine of Virtue* by German philosopher Immanuel Kant, in order to do our imperfect obligations, we must be able to control our inclinations and dispositions, which are constantly at odds with the moral law.

Judeo-Christian

The Old and New Testament of the Bible, the sacred literature of adherents of both Judaism and Christianity, promote and teach Judeo-Christian ideals. The Ten Commandments and the two volumes of Proverbs, which notably advise on the repercussions of virtues and vices, are two passages of the Old Testament that are particularly indicative of values valued by Jewish culture and Christians. Proverbs promotes virtues like honesty, decency, righteousness, humility, and dependability. Character development is thought to occur through adversity and steadfastness in the Christian faith.

Islam

The Qu'ran, the Muslim bible, serves as the source for Muslims' moral precepts. Humility, modesty, restraint of impulses, and integrity are only a few of the virtues upheld by the Qur'an.

Confucianism

The five main virtues espoused by Confucianism are *jen* (also known as humanity, human-heartedness, or benevolence), *yi* (also known as duty, justice, or equity), *li* (also known as etiquette or observing the rites of ceremonious behavior), *zhi* (also known as wisdom or perspicacity), and *xin* (also known as truthfulness, sincerity, or good faith).

Buddhism

Buddhism teaches that the Eightfold Path's philosophy and approach are known to call upon the fundamental virtues of humanity, justice, temperance, transcendence, and knowledge. Nirvana is described as the ultimate goal of existence.

Hinduism

Hinduism places a strong focus on personal characteristics like self-denial and renunciation because they help people improve themselves in this life and have the possibility to be saved or rise to a higher caste in the afterlife.

Character Development

Ancient thinkers believed that character is developed by repeated actions that are either rewarded or by learning through experience. According to their theory, a variety of different habits that can both enable and constrain us and that can be both productive and destructive are created along with the habit of character. We frequently aren't even conscious of our habits, which is an interesting fact about them. Lao Tzu, a Chinese philosopher, is credited with stating, "Watch your ideas, for they become words," which serves as a good example of this idea. Keep an eye on your words since they become deeds. Watch your behavior because it develops into habits. Watch your habits, because they shape your personality. Watch your character; it will determine your fate.

Character development is the process through which an individual's personality emerges from the opportunities provided by nature and within the confines of environmental or cultural circumstances. However, character is also a singular accomplishment that is a result of an individual's creativity, work, and desire. Environmental and cultural influences are taken into consideration in psychological approaches to character formation.

The development of excellent character is also influenced by close ties to family and friends. For instance, sibling connections give kids the chance to practice social intelligence and problem-solving techniques, two character qualities.

Biological Influences

Nature vs. nurture. Morality is a function of both our biology (our nature) and our experiences, like any other human ability (nurture). We develop moral character as a result of the interaction between our innate propensity for empathy and the affection we receive from our parents. This is seen in the behavior of six- and seven-year-old children, who can distinguish between right and evil and feel guilty when engaging in immoral behaviors.

Character development also involves the development of temperament and personality. Studies on temperament have revealed the ways in which physiologically based individual differences in sociability, emotionality, and activity level influence later personality development. Empathic tendencies and prosocial behavioral patterns are heritable, according to twin studies of both adults and children.

We must "fight our tendency to make right or accurate that which is only familiar and erroneous or untrue that which is merely strange," according to psychologist Robert Kegan. Character can influence how we think, speak, and behave. But undesirable habits and conduct may impede character formation. For instance, a large ego makes it challenging to cultivate humility and subsequently be open to learning or various viewpoints.

The characteristics and values that make up character are greatly influenced by important life events. Some of these occurrences make people face the consequences of their trait- and value-driven activities as well as the virtue of their character. Events that can affect character include being fired, receiving positive or negative feedback on your work, being passed over for a promotion or getting one when you didn't think you were ready, suffering the consequences of a boss's unfair evaluation, and being accused of harassment, plagiarism, or other unethical behavior.

Character development is extremely important, especially in young children, and depends on people receiving notice, praise, recognition, or rewards for doing the right thing or acting in the right way.

Character development can happen as a result of commonplace occurrences and circumstances because it is an integral aspect of one's life and work. When those situations arise, introspection on the reasons you might be impatient, overly stubborn, or thoughtless gives the foundation for character analysis and development.

The Aristotelian idea of character is supported by moral educationist Thomas Lickona. He makes the case that morality is manifested in behavior, and that people develop in morality as a value develops into a virtue or a dependable inner inclination. The development of character happens in this way.

According to certain psychological theories, character is the culmination of the attributes or routines needed to lead a successful life. According to psychotherapist Raymond Corsini, character refers to a person's overall attributes or features, especially those that are distinctive of their moral, social, and religious perspectives. Character is defined by positive attributes that have arisen throughout history and throughout cultures as being crucial for leading a happy life. Character is also said to be made up of traits like social responsibility, moral commitment, self-control, and tenacity, depending on which combination of traits the individual is assessed to possess. Others view character as an outward manifestation of one's moral compass, resolve, conscience, and principles.

Psychological Influences

The formation of good character is influenced by many different factors. The authoritative parenting style, which has continuously been linked to children's prosocial behaviors like sharing with peers, self-control, and self-assurance, is one such influence.

Second, prosocial behaviors like sharing, assisting, and being a good teammate are known to be facilitated by positive role modelling and appropriate reward. Due to the operant and cognitive principles at play, which are demonstrated by other people's behavior, reinforcement, and the usage of rewards, social observational learning happens. The development of excellent character is also influenced by close ties to family and friends. For instance, sibling connections give kids the chance to practice social intelligence and problem-solving techniques, two character qualities. Moral reasoning is improved by moral instruction in schools, especially among high school pupils.

It is also possible to approach moral formation from a cultural-social perspective or paradigm. Nearly all cultures include education and "rites of passage" that are meant to shape a child's character into a devoted and useful citizen.

This situation is also relevant to Kohlberg's theory of moral development. According to Kohlberg, moral reasoning progresses through six recognisable phases and the majority of moral development happens through social contact. His approach concentrated on the maturation of cognitive functions, particularly the justification of duties, rights, and justice. According to Kohlberg, most adults never go to stage six of moral development. Respect for universal standards and social conscience requirements define this stage. Through social connection, cognitive struggle, a supportive moral climate, and democratic engagement, moral development can be enhanced in the classroom. The perspective of lifespan developmental psychology on development is consistent with Kohlberg's contention that change and transformation occur continuously over the course of progressively complex systems or stages. Adults are expected to demonstrate morality that is more complex and integrated, yet not all adults exhibit the same levels of "moral maturity."

Final Thoughts and Questions to Consider

This chapter has presented a description from ancient to modern times, traits and characteristics of good character. The list is long, but comprehensive.

1. When you think of leaders of great good character, who comes to mind? What were the qualities they exhibited?

2. If you were responsible for hiring or promoting a leader, what kinds of questions would you ask them?

Chapter 2

Core Values and Self-Identity

"Your core values are the deeply held beliefs that authentically describe your soul."

— John C. Maxwell

I n my book, *I Know Myself and Neither Do You*, I go into detail on how the foundation of effective leadership is self-awareness. "We need to regularly reflect upon our core beliefs if we are to live a meaningful life where our values and beliefs are in sync with our actions," I contend. We can address the issue of self-deception with the use of this approach. Our desire to engage "in objective self-examination and also accept whatever personal inadequacies" that may be revealed by that self-examination process poses the challenge in knowing ourselves.

Our desire to examine ourselves involves both self-assurance and humility. Additionally, it enables us to evaluate the discrepancy between our own evaluations and those of others more precisely.

Clarifying and comprehending our underlying ideas is crucial, as is taking self-correcting action, which includes the crucial step of realizing how we lie to ourselves, according to researcher Lawrence Ackerman.

He contends that in order to have an accurate perspective on the world, we must be aware of our own biases and how they affect how we perceive the world. According to Ackerman, self-identity, self-awareness, and self-deception all give us the chance to improve our comprehension of the moral obligations entailed by interpersonal connections. Organizations may strengthen connections, develop commitment and trust, and improve organizational outcomes by understanding how identity, self-awareness, and self-deception relate in a business environment.

What is "The Self?"

Finding one's "real" self, which is expressed through self-coherence, self-identification, and self-actualization, is a common topic in psychology. Psychologists primarily neglected the self until the late 20th century, with a few prominent exceptions (William James, neo-Freudians, and humanists). The ego did not become a topic of discussion until after behaviorism and psychoanalysis fell out of fashion.

On the other hand, self-analysis has a long tradition in philosophy. We have the *Tao Te Ching*, the *Upanishads,* and the Buddha's teachings in the East. In the West, Plato was followed by religious philosophers who focused on the sinful aspects of the ego before the Enlightenment. Several philosophers, including Descartes, Locke, Hume, Leibnitz, Berkeley, and Kant, wrote about the self during the Enlightenment. Since then, there has been ongoing debate among philosophers on the nature of the self, also known as "the problem of the self," which includes inquiries like: Is there a self? How are we to know? What does the self in self-awareness look like? What connection exists between the self and the brain?

Since Descartes, abstract contemplation has been the dominant mode of thought in the West, dividing subject and object, oneself and others, and oneself and the world of objects (this is often referred to as dualism).

This tradition bases the idea of a distinct "I" entity on psychological frameworks or schemas. As a result, Western psychology adopted the formation of a stable and robust ego as a goal.

Contrarily, self-reflection is seen in the West as embodied, aware, and receptive to the ever-changing nature of bodily sensations that do not imply an autonomous self that engages in that contemplation. This is due to the impact of Eastern philosophy and religion. Instead, the observer merges with the reflective experience, and the reflection itself takes on the nature of an experience. It is a fully embodied condition of being that is defined by "self-letting go and letting be," awareness and acceptance of body feeling, and non-attachment. In this approach, self-awareness is viewed as a tool to change and advance personally.

We have been taught to think that our thoughts and everything else that is hidden beneath the skin make up our "selves." However, some would contend that it only makes up a minor portion of what is concealed. Cognitive neuroscientists estimate that only 5% of your daily cognitive activity consists of conscious thoughts. The other 95% of brain activity is not visible to the human mind. It would be like identifying oneself only based on your conscious thoughts after just having answered five of a math test with 100 problems.

Awareness of Oneself and Identity

Identity also includes those fundamental, persistent, and distinctive characteristics of an individual at the personal or individual level. Identity has been conceptualized at the organizational level as including the core, persistent, and distinctive characteristics of an organization.

Our identity is inversely correlated to how we act, the roles we play, and how closely our actions match our idealized ideal behavior.

In contrast to one's identification as a distinctive individual identity at the personal level, social identity deals with one's perceived function as a member of a group. It is associated with individual identity. Comparing oneself to others and verifying one's identity in light of how one thinks others view them serve to legitimize this.

We employ the complex process of self-evaluation to guide our actions in accordance with who we think we are. This process usually takes place at the unconscious and sub-conscious levels. In order to determine our self-image and identities, we evaluate ourselves in relation to people who are both similar to us and different from us. Our self-perceptions and the characteristics that define our social and personal identities may be integrated.

Self-awareness involves our level of sensitivity to how others view us, whereas identification reveals who we think we are. According to research on self-awareness, persons who are more aware of how others see them are better at incorporating that knowledge into their self-appraisals and, consequently, into their conduct.

When it comes to identification and self-awareness and leadership effectiveness, a leader's awareness of how their followers see them has significant ramifications. For instance, research has shown that leaders are more effective when they exhibit an openness to criticism from others, even when it is unfavorable.

There is a clear link between enhanced self-awareness and character and virtous behavior. Leaders who are not self-aware may be blind to the consequences of their actions that harm others, or blind to their motivations for doing so. So their primary character trait can be seen as ego-driven, self-serving and insensitive the needs of others. In contrast, the self-aware leader regularly reflects on the motivations for behaviors and can understand the possible negative impact on the welfare of others.

Values

What are the tenets or convictions that guide your life? What do you believe in? What would you die for or make sacrifices for? Our values can be used to define the response to such queries.

Values are the guiding principles and expectations that guide us through life. Our convictions serve as our guide for what is morally upright or deserving. Values act as a compass inside of us. The degree to which a person's behavior is congruent with their professed values is known as value congruence. Honesty, integrity, friendship, family, challenge, harmony, compassion, and loyalty are a few examples of values.

Great leaders are confident and clear about their values and how they influence their actions and choices. Leaders' values need to be clarified in two steps: identifying their core principles and clearly expressing them to others through their words and deeds.

Professors Ian C. Woodward and Sanah Shaffakat of the INSEAD Advanced Management Program created the integrated model of a personal values system known as *Understanding Values for Insightfully Aware Leaders.* They discovered in their study of 163 owners, senior, and middle managers that executives' values had a direct and significant impact on organizational performance, although age, tenure, experience, and education did not. According to other studies, values have an effect on employee dedication, productivity, and performance.

By enabling leaders to reflect on what is most important to them and use that understanding to guide subsequent decisions, behaviors, and relationships, values identification and clarity can have a positive impact on leaders' self-awareness.

Self-awareness is necessary for self-identity. It involves making a decision of some sort. For instance, you might support GreenPeace because you care deeply about preserving our world, while you may be interested in charity because you want to aid the less fortunate. Although we are born with personality features, we do not have an identity. It changes and advances with time.

Everyone has a perception of themselves and a notion about their personal identity. Security comes from a solid sense of identity. We spend a lot of time as children trying to figure out what we believe, what we want, and who we are.

Some of us have what is known as a "midlife crisis" in which we realize we are not who we thought we were over the previous ten, twenty, or even thirty years. This typically occurs when we accomplish a significant goal only to discover that it hasn't left us feeling as content or pleased as we had anticipated.

How Do Values Influence Our Self-Identity?

People develop a sense of consistency in their identity as they become older and their values become clearer. Usually, our beliefs or principles are the driving force behind our decisions and behaviors. In other words, our self-identity includes our values. In the process of exploring and uncovering our beliefs, we get to understand who we truly are.

There are ten different value categories, according to S.H. Schwartz and W. Bilsky in their article published in the *Journal of Personality and Social Psychology*: generosity, universalism (equality, environmental protection), security, tradition (honesty, respect), conformity, power (dominance, authority), achievement (ambition, personal success), self-direction (creativity, independent thought), hedonism (the pursuit of pleasure), and stimulation (having a rich, exciting life). Achievement-related values can be found in a person's employment status, job title, and pay.

Our self-identity may reflect how we view the ideal mate or family (e.g.: a person sees themselves as primarily a parent or mother). Under the veneer of presentability, traditional strong motivations like sex, power, and money can be found. Politics, religion, philosophy, and worldview all have an impact on how we live and do determine who we are.

How Do Identities Change?

Assuming our values are consistent with who we truly are, thinking and acting in accordance with our values can help us lead more fulfilling lives. Abraham Maslow and Carl Rogers, both psychologists, put out the key ideas pertaining to self-concept. According to Maslow's hierarchy of needs, those who are able to reach the level of self-actualization at the top of the scale live or make an effort to live completely in accordance with their ideals. According to psychologist Carl Rogers, people want to act, feel, and experience things that are consistent with their "ideal selves," or ideas of who they want to be. They act, feel, and think in these ways in a way that is congruent with their "real-self."

Ideal self, self-esteem, and self-image are the three components that make up one's self-concept. We believe we should be our ideal selves. Self-esteem is an emotional evaluation of who we are. Lastly, our perception of ourselves is our self-image.

According to literature on leadership and psychology, a leader's essential beliefs and values form the basis of their character. The cognitive frameworks that affect leaders' knowledge of moral and ethical dilemmas, judgement, intentions, and moral and ethical action are their core values and beliefs. Over time, followers might deduce the fundamental principles and beliefs of leaders by observing their actions. Leaders exhibit the possession of such enduring virtues as honesty, integrity, courage, compassion, and humility by their deeds. As a result, they are more likely to receive positive character references from their supporters. In turn, followers' assessments of leaders' moral integrity contribute to the growth of trust, which increases followers' readiness to cooperate and support the leader.

The more important a leader's core values and beliefs are to who they are as a person, the more morally aware they are, which in turn leads to more consistently moral and ethical behavior. Such leaders are inwardly driven to act morally and ethically because they think it is the right thing to do and because it helps them stay true to who they are as people. Additionally, leaders who are still in the early phases of this integration process are still very vulnerable to external motivational factors, such as monetary incentive and status, which affect the consistency of moral and ethical behavior. Therefore, character development and consistent moral and ethical behavior in all situations appear to depend on leaders' ability to integrate their values and belief systems with their self-identities.

Leaders will constantly come across circumstances that pose moral conundrums. Leaders must take action to overcome the ethical conundrum once they have decided what the appropriate moral response to a given circumstance is. Sometimes, leaders are aware of the proper conduct but do not follow it, leaving the ethical conundrum unresolved. Sean Hannah and Bruce Avoli argue in their article in the *Leadership Quarterly* that the "moral potency" of leaders explains the discrepancy between knowing what is morally correct and inspiring people to act morally. Moral potency is characterized as a psychological state in which leaders feel a sense of agency over the moral facets of their environment, have faith in their ability to carry out the conduct, and have the moral fortitude to act in the face of difficulty. It gives executives the psychological tools they need to go from moral reflection to moral and ethical action.

Final Thoughts and Questions to Consider

This chapter has focused on the connection between values, self-identity and character. How leaders show up in the world, and the behaviors they exhibit often reflects what they value most. Also, having a clear sense of their identity and good self-awareness will allow them to make decisions and take actions there are alignment.

Here Are Some Questions to Consider:

1. What practices can leaders engage in to raise their self-awareness?

2. What process can leaders use to ensure their values, identity and desired leadership character are in alignment?

3. Should there be a process in organizations where leaders personal values are contrasted to the organization's values to uncover any dissonance?

Chapter 3

Character Strengths and Leader Character

"People will not follow a leader with moral incongruities for long. Every time you compromise character you compromise leadership. The foundation of firm leadership is character."

— Winston Churchill

Since the inception of the positive psychology movement, character strengths have been at its core. "Researchers have discovered that there are human strengths that act as buffers against mental illness," Martin Seligman and Mihalyi Csikszentmihalyi write in their article on the field's introduction in the *American Psychologist*. "These strengths include courage, future-mindedness, optimism, interpersonal skill, faith, work ethic, hope, honesty, perseverance, and the capacity for flow and insight, to name a few. The creation of a science of human strengths, whose goal it is to comprehend and learn how to promote these values in young people, will take up a significant portion of the prevention effort in this new century."

Do values and character traits differ in any way? In *A Primer in Positive Psychology*, Christopher Peterson says that values are beliefs that people and groups hold about desirable ends. They direct how we choose our activities and judge others and ourselves, and they are ranked according to their relative importance. Character strengths can be used by individuals to further their particular values.

Positive attributes that are consistently praised for the strength they instill in people are known as character strengths. They can be seen in a person's ideas, feelings, and behaviors.

Character traits, positive relationships, happy experiences, and positive institutions are all part of the scientific study of what makes life the most worthwhile.

Although it emphasizes the good things in life, positive psychology does not downplay the negative. In *Character Strengths and Virtues: A Handbook and Classification* by Peterson and Seligman, they state "It's tempting to think of positive psychology as focusing on stress-free people, but this is incorrect .We cannot dismiss the negative while highlighting the positive. We must consider conditions of difficulty while talking about character strengths, whether they are internal or external." Petersen and Seligman outlined a number of standards for character strengths:

1. They must support the pursuits that make up the "happy life" for oneself or others.

2. They have moral significance in and of itself, even in the absence of favorable results.

3. One person's demonstration of power does not reduce those around him or her.

4. They don't clearly have a negative "opposite."

5. They must show up in a fashion that can be evaluated and be at least somewhat consistent over time and circumstances.

6. They cannot be supplanted by another strength and is separate from other positive characteristics included in the classification system.

7. They can be demonstrated by "paragons," or individuals with exceptional levels of strength.

8. Someone may possess an innate aptitude for it and be a "prodigy" in it.

9. There are "institutions and accompanying rituals" for growing it, indicating that at least some sectors of mainstream society view it favorably and actively foster it.

The writers identified six basic qualities that manifested in communities throughout history and the world using these criteria. There are numerous character strengths related to exhibiting or practicing the virtue in each of these qualities. Here is how they categorized character traits.*

1. **Knowledge and Wisdom:** The acquisition of convictions, even if they are unpopular; this encompasses but is not limited to physical bravery.

   • Endurance, perseverance: Finishing what one begins; continuing in a line of action despite difficulties; "getting it out the door"; enjoying task completion.

   • Logic and rationality.

2. **Honesty:** Not telling lies or falsehoods.

   • Genuineness.

- Integrity

- Speaking the truth, but more broadly, behaving sincere and presenting oneself that way.

- Having no pretense..

- Assuming accountability for one's thoughts and deeds.

3. **Humanity:** Social skills that include taking care of and befriending others.

    - Love: Appreciating close relationships with others, especially ones in which sharing and caring are reciprocated; being near others.

    - Generosity: (also known as nurturing, caring, compassion, altruistic love, or "niceness"):

    - Doing good deeds and favors for other people; looking out for them; and providing for their needs.

    - Social intelligence: Also known as emotional intelligence or personal intelligence, is the capacity to understand one's own and others' motivations and feelings, as well as to adapt to various social contexts and understand how others function.

4. **Justice:** Civic virtues that support a strong sense of community.

    - Citizenship: commitment to others, fidelity, and cooperation.

- Being a team player or group player effectively.

- Fairness: Treating everyone equally in accordance with ideals of justice and fairness.

- Making decisions without letting personal feelings influence them.

- Offering each person an equal chance.

5. **Temperance:** The capacity to withstand excess.

   - Mercy and forgiveness.

   - Acknowledging other people's flaws.

   - Not seeking revenge.

   - Let one's accomplishments speak for themselves with humility and modesty.

   - Prudence is the quality of making wise decisions.

   - Avoiding unnecessary risks.

   - Self-control and self-regulation.

6. **Transcendence:** Attributes that provide links to the greater cosmos and offer purpose.

   - Awe, wonder, and elevation: the appreciation of quality and beauty.

   - Observing and enjoying beauty, excellence, and/or skillful performance in a variety of spheres of existence, including ordinary life, nature, art, mathematics, and science.

- Being mindful of and appreciative for the positive things that occur.

- Taking the time to offer gratitude.

- Hope: optimism, a focus on the future, a future-oriented attitude.

- Believing that one can influence the future for the better.

- Spirituality: religiosity, belief, and goal.

- Holding views that are consistent with the universe's larger meaning and purpose.

- Understanding one's place in the bigger picture.

*Adapted from: *Character Strengths and Virtues: A Handbook and Classification* by Martin E. P. Seligman and Christopher Peterson.

Strengths of Character for Leaders

Character strengths are psychological characteristics that support, develop, and communicate character in three key ways. First, leaders help others integrate their basic values and beliefs into their self-identities by drawing on their character strengths. The character strength of self-awareness, for example, is used by leaders to integrate their core values and beliefs with their self-concepts by routinely reflecting on and evaluating the basic beliefs and values by which they define themselves.

Second, leaders can make use of their moral judgement prowess to guarantee that their actions are consistent with the principles and beliefs that make them who they are. For instance, a business executive who regards integrity as a vital value might have to decide how to distribute bonuses equitably among personnel. The boss would have to use the character strength of self-regulation to restrain the impulse of greed and ensure fair distribution of bonuses among the personnel in order to ensure that his decisions are applied honestly and consistently.

The leader may also utilize his social awareness EQ quality to predict how the workforce would likely respond to his decisions. In order to make sure that decisions about bonus distribution are consistent with the leader's guiding principle of justice or fairness, the leader makes use of two character strengths.

A leader's character traits can be used to show people what they believe and value most. For instance, a military leader who refuses to follow a directive from higher headquarters because it unnecessarily endangers the lives of soldiers not only exemplifies the virtue of bravery in action, but also conveys to others that they value courage above all else.

Based on interviews with more than 2,500 leaders from North America, Europe, Asia, and Latin America, Gerard H. Seijts and Jeffrey Gandz, writing in *Business Horizons,* offered a framework for defining a leader's character. According to the framework, there are 11 elements of a leader's character that have an independent and reciprocal impact on organizational and individual outcomes.

The 11 characteristics of a leader's character and their significance for transformation are:

1. Courage: bravery, tenacity, determination, and confidence.

2. Accountability: ownership, acceptance of responsibility, diligence, and responsibility.

3. Justice: fairness, equity, proportionality, balance, and social responsibility.

4. Temperance: self-control, restraint, serenity, and patience.

5. Integrity: genuineness, forthrightness, openness, morality, and consistency.

6. Humility: awareness of oneself, modesty, reflection, curiosity, respect, gratitude, and vulnerability.

7. Humanity: considerate, empathetic, compassionate, magnanimous, kind, generous, and forgiving.

8. Collaboration: cooperative, collegial, open-minded, flexible, interconnected.

9. Drive: enthusiastic, active, results-oriented, shows initiative, and aspires to greatness.

10. Transcendence: appreciative, inspired, purposive, optimistic, creative, future-oriented.

11. Judgment: situationally aware, analytical, decisive, intuitive, insightful, pragmatic, adaptive.

Leadership Capability

When the subject of leadership development is brought up, the emphasis is frequently on boldness, organizational skills, vision, strategy, and planning. But today, without the fundamental leadership characteristic of high character, none of that will result in a great leader.

Effective leadership is built on a foundation of strong character because people will follow a leader they can trust. Obviously, one cannot lead without followers.

However, in this day of individuality, we seldom ever discuss the qualities of excellent character. A leader of good character is someone who scored highly on integrity, responsibility, compassion, and forgiveness, according to Fred Kiel's definition in his book *Return on Character*. When we consider a leader with questionable morals — someone who avoids taking personal responsibility, is dishonest and untrustworthy, and lacks sympathy and empathy — Kiel's assessment becomes evident.

One of the traits of a leader with high character is their ability to be trusted. What therefore constitutes someone as trustworthy? What Kiel suggests is this:

- They follow through on their commitments, or they do what they say they'll do.

- They have demonstrated consistency over time, which makes their behavior dependable behavior and reactions to comparable circumstances.

- They are sincere and truthful.

- They are courageous in that they always act in accordance with what is right, even when it is challenging, and they make well-considered decisions by being receptive to advice and the opinions of others.

- Rather than only pursuing their own interests, they look out for the interests of others.

Organizational psychologist Fred Kiel has spent four decades providing advice to senior executives and was initially surprised by how few of them, despite being "very principled," showed concern for the general welfare. This was not because they were against the concept; rather, it was because they were "focused only on what was good for their specific business." He was surprised by his executive clients' apparent lack of understanding of "the fundamental levers for creating value," as well. Kiel said "they had "ittle concept that who they are" as being "just as vital as what they know how to do," and they "usually undervalued approaches for inspiring and energizing the workforce."

In *Return on Character,* he and his colleagues sought to ascertain whether an executive's character could be developed and improved during their career, how thoroughly it could be assessed, and how directly it might be tied to an organization's bottom line.

As much as five times the amount of return on assets can be demonstrated by Kiel for good character leaders compared to those at the weaker end of the spectrum. Such leadership is also associated with much higher levels of employee engagement.

His second finding is that a lot of what makes up strong character can be acquired through developing positive leadership character practices and modifying negative ones.

Kiel and his research team at KRW International, the Minneapolis-based consultancy he co-founded to increase leadership effectiveness, believe that much about a leader's character can be inferred "by how they treat people in the workplace," especially where there is no obvious gain to themselves. They drew on the extensive comparative literature on human ethics to develop a "strong framework for a principled approach to leadership" based on the following four principles:

According to Kiel, actions that show integrity, such as being truthful and standing up for what is right, aid in building trust; responsibility, such as taking ownership of one's own decisions and mistakes, tend to be motivating; and forgiveness, such as continuing to place more emphasis on encouraging others than placing blame; and compassion and empathy, are both fundamental building blocks of empowerment. Kiel's framework for evaluating character strength in action is based on these "keystone character habits," two of the head (integrity and responsibility) and two of the heart (forgiveness and compassion).

Based on how frequently they were observed exhibiting the behaviors connected to the four core character habits, the KRW team utilized this method to profile the character strengths of 84 U.S. CEOs. They then arranged them on a "character curve" to represent their character strengths. The difference between the ten "virtuoso CEOs" at the top and the ten "self-focused CEOs" near the bottom was then their main point of emphasis.

Self-awareness was one of the most glaring distinctions between the high character leaders and their self-focused rivals. When self-ratings on the cornerstone qualities were compared to those of their subordinates, high character leaders were found to be "pretty accurate in their self-awareness." Contrarily, the majority of self-centered CEOs "dramatically overrated their demonstration of moral habits" in comparison to the ratings of their staff and were prone to significant self-deception, which ultimately hurt the business performance of the firm and, in some cases, even put the firm's survival at risk.

As Kiel notes, self-awareness is "essential equipment for the job" when it comes to leadership, and the majority of the self-focused CEOs who lack it run the risk of staying in a condition of "arrested progress." In contrast, leaders who actively pursue greater self-awareness, according to Kiel, are better able to critically evaluate "not only the ideas of others" but also their "own most cherished beliefs," and as a result, their comprehension of their daily lives, their businesses, their markets, and the external forces that influence them "enters a state of continual growth and development."

Other Leader Character Descriptions. Other authors have listed the following qualities as characteristics of good character: kindness, humility, humor, integrity, patience, perseverance, fidelity, honesty, temperance, justice, patience, industry, truth, respect, responsibility, fairness, caring, dignity, trustworthiness, calmness, and fairness.

The historical figures whose personalities we tend to admire the most as leaders have earned the esteem and loyalty of their followers. Today's followers are looking for role models who not only exhibit the skills required for effective leadership, but also display integrity, courage, compassion, and service. Character conveys reliability, potential, and deference to followers. The good character of leaders can therefore be emulated by followers, strengthening the organization and its bottom line by inexorably fostering character development at all organizational levels.

The relationship between character traits, virtues, and happiness was thoroughly investigated by Denise Quinlan, Nicola Swain, and Dianne A. Vella-Brodrick in their article published in the *Journal of Happiness Studies.* They also looked at the effects of lacking leadership virtues.

They claim that if you think about what might occur when leaders lack these qualities, the repercussions become more apparent. They argue the following:

- **Without good judgment** leaders frequently make poor decisions, particularly when they must respond fast in unclear circumstances, such as when they are presented with the numerous paradoxes that occasionally face all leaders.

- **Without humanity,** leaders are unable to empathize with others, view things from the perspectives of their followers, or consider how their decisions may affect other people. Without humanity, leaders will act in ways that alienate people rather than in ways that are socially responsible.

- **Without a sense of justice** leaders are unable to comprehend the problems with social inequality and the difficulties of fairness without a sense of justice. Such leaders take unjust measures that result in poor employee relations or negative responses from the public, the government, and regulators. People will resist and try to remove the leader in various ways.

- **Without courage**, leaders will be unable to confront others' poor choices and will lack the tenacity and determination needed to resolve challenging problems. In addition, when faced with difficulty, they will back down and take the simple path. But they only delay what will happen as a result.

- **Without collaboration,** leaders will be unable to accomplish important objectives that call for more than just one person's abilities and commitment. They don't make better decisions or carry them out better by utilizing the diversity of knowledge, experience, views, judgments, and talents of others. Relations worsen as a result of friction between various interests.

- **Without accountability,** leaders cannot persuade people to commit to or take ownership of their decisions. They create a culture of fear and disengagement by blaming others for bad outcomes. People cease caring, which could have terrible repercussions.

- **Without humility,** leaders are unable to be open-minded, solicit, and take into account the opinions of others. They are unable to grow as leaders as a result of reflecting critically on their mistakes and learning from those of others. They resemble cartoon versions of themselves. It leads to isolation.

- **Without integrity,** leaders are unable to forge strong bonds with subordinates and superiors within their organizations, or external allies, or partners. Every assurance must be provided, which causes mistrust and slows down choices and actions.

- **Without temperance** leaders take unwise risks, jump to conclusions, neglect to obtain relevant information, lack perspective, make frequent and detrimental changes, and even go back on crucial decisions. They lose credibility.

- **Without transcendence,** leaders' objectives become constrained and they are unable to move conversations to higher-order objectives. They lack perspective, thus their choices might merely be motivated by opportunism. They don't inspire others to think creatively or unconventionally.

Virtue	Good Organizational Outcomes (Virtue is present)	Bad Organizational Outcomes (Virtue is absent)
Judgment	Quality decision; calculated risk-taking; commitment; support, trust;	Lack of a balanced assessment of the issues leading to misinformed decisions; confusion; resistance to change.
Humanity	Social responsibility; good employee relations; understanding, support.	Misses critical social implications of decisions and actions; alienation of followers; lack of respect for the leader.
Justice	Use of diversity; good employee relations;	Inequities not identified and managed thereby

	fairness, organizational citizenship behaviors.	eroding trust; favoritism, nepotism.
Courage	Decisions made under conditions of uncertainty, confidence to act; opposition to potentially bad decisions; innovation.	Going along with poor decisions; satisficing rather than maximizing; moral muteness.
Collaboration	Teamwork; cross-enterprise value-added; innovation; learning; confidence.	Individualism alienates potential allies; poor understanding of decisions; friction; conflict.
Accountability	Ownership and commitment to decisions and their execution.	Failure to deliver results and typically creates excuses for why not; shirking of responsibly; blaming others.
Humility	Continuous learning; quality decisions; respect; trust; not ego-driven; service.	Hubris; selective listening; difficulty admitting mistakes or failure; overconfidence; complacency.
Integrity	Builds trust; reduces uncertainty; develops	Creates mistrust; requires personal

	partnerships and alliances; promotes collaboration and cooperation.	loyalty; procrastinates; undermines partnerships and alliances; not cooperative and collaborative.
Temperance	Quality decisions; reduced risk; non-impulsiveness; patience.	Short-termism; inability to see the possible constraints; instant gratification; impulsiveness.
Transcendence	Focus on superordinate goals; big-picture thinking; strive for excellence; integration with social good.	Narrow aims; little inspiration, tunnel vision.

Figure 2: Adapted from Quinlan et al. (2012)

Final Thoughts and Questions to Consider

A leader's character strengths can often be a seen in the daily actions the leader takes, particularly in conflict situations or ethical decisions to be made.

Here are some questions to consider:

1. What are your character strengths? Are they transparent to others?

2. How do your character strengths relate to your most important personal values? Your organization's values?

3. When have your character strengths been tested in an ethical situation? What was the result?

Chapter 4

Virtues and Virtuous Leadership

"The virtue of a person is measured not by his outstanding efforts, but by his everyday behavior."

— Blaise Pascal

A person's moral perfection, or a morally righteous inclination to think, feel, and act rightly, is referred to as virtue. A vice, on the other hand, is a morally repugnant attitude that involves negative thinking, feeling, and behavior. Characteristics known as virtues are essential to a person's personality. A virtue is a quality that makes the person who possesses it good; a vice, on the other hand, makes the person who possesses it bad. As a result, leaders can be viewed as "good" or "bad" depending on their virtues or lack thereof.

Phronesis, a word from Greek that means "prudence," "a practical virtue," or "practical wisdom," is an acquired quality that aids a person in making the best decision in any scenario. Practical reason, as contrast to theoretical wisdom, leads to action or choice. Practical wisdom demands "perceptual sensitivity," as John McDowell claims in his piece in *The Monist*, to what a circumstance calls for.

Greek words for *eudaimonia* include "well-being," "happiness," "blessedness," and, in the context of virtue ethics, "human flourishing." Eudaimonia, in Aristotle's view, is the proper objective of human life.

Socrates laid the foundation for virtue ethics, which were later refined by Plato, Aristotle, and the Stoics. A group of normative ethical theories that emphasize being rather than doing are referred to as virtue ethics.

Another way to put this is to argue that morality in virtue ethics is derived from the identity or character of the individual rather than being a result of their actions. What specific virtues are morally laudable now is a topic of discussion among different virtue ethics adherents.

However, the majority of thinkers concur that innate virtues lead to morality. The way qualities are viewed by Plato and Aristotle differs. According to Plato, virtue is essentially a goal to be pursued through practical means. According to Aristotle, virtues serve primarily as safeguards for interpersonal relationships.

In Plato's *Republic,* the so-called "four cardinal virtues"—wisdom, justice, fortitude, and temperance—are discussed. The virtues play a significant role in Aristotle's *Nicomachean Ethics* moral philosophy as well. Moralistic historians like Livy, Plutarch, and Tacitus introduced virtue theory to history as a way to better understand the past. The Roman philosopher Cicero introduced the Greek concept of the virtues, which St. Ambrose of Milan later incorporated into the Christian moral theology. The *Summa Theologiae,* written by St. Thomas Aquinas, is the most in-depth theological analysis of the virtues to date. Aristotle's *Nicomachean Ethics* remained the primary source for the study of ethics at Protestant universities after the Reformation up until the late seventeenth century.

During this time, the word "virtue" was still in use; in fact, it plays a significant role in the classical republican or classical liberal traditions. The term "virtue" is used frequently in the writings of Niccol Machiavelli, David Hume, the republicans of the English Civil War era, the English Whigs of the 18th century, and the notable figures among the Scottish Enlightenment and the American Founding Fathers. This tradition was significant in the intellectual life of 16th-century Italy as well as 17th- and 18th-century Britain and America.

Twelve virtues—courage, temperance, generosity, magnificence, magnanimity, right aspiration, good temper, friendliness, honesty, wit, and justice—were named and described by Aristotle. Practical Wisdom, the twelfth virtue, is essential to leading the "good life" and achieving happiness or well-being.

Take the attribute of courage as an example. Individuals who uphold ideals like integrity, treating others with respect, and success are more likely to act bravely. Even though both people are in the same scenario, a person with integrity will typically behave differently from a person without integrity. Then there are a selection of actual behaviors that people exhibit on a regular basis (i.e., in a variety of circumstances and over time), which friends, coworkers, and outside observers categorize or describe as courageous. It's possible that these actions have evolved into societal norms.

Strengths Evaluations and Classifications of Virtues

There are many descriptions of virtues by different authors, as well as tests to see if you possess such virtues.

The Values in Action (VIA) Inventory of Character Strengths, Realise 2, and StrengthsFinder and the Virtues Project (VPA) are four categories for virtue strengths. These characteristics have influenced the intervention tactics and outcomes measurements employed with these classifications since they differ in their origins, objectives, strength definitions, and nomenclature. For instance, The VIA Inventory of Character Strengths defines psychological or character strengths as morally desirable traits whose use adds to fulfilment and enjoyment. This definition is based on a survey of historically and now generally recognized character traits.

Interventions based on The Inventory's 24-strength classification first aimed to gauge how these strengths were developing and how they affected overall wellbeing. In contrast, StrengthsFinder was created to help professional achievement and personal growth and is based on empirical workplace research of talents that can be developed into strengths. Both classifications promote identifying a person's top five or "signature strengths" and share the definitional hunch that focusing on one's strengths rather than flaws results in better benefits for the individual. This feature of the definition of strengths has helped intervention efforts to concentrate on utilizing top strengths.

The 100 virtues identified by The Virtues Project (TVP), in contrast, aim to encourage the usage of all the virtues in order to encourage good conduct and wellbeing. Realise2 identifies 60 strengths and groups them into realized and unfulfilled strengths, learned behaviors, and shortcomings for the respondents. Realise2 places an emphasis on performance ability, the energy an individual obtains from using strengths, and how frequently the strength is used. It was developed based on workplace observations of high performance and is largely used in the office and in coaching. In contrast to the other categories, respondents are made aware of their limitations and urged to think about where to best concentrate their development efforts, whether those efforts should be directed toward developing strengths or weaknesses.

According to one definition of psychological strengths, they are "means of acting, thinking, or feeling that an individual has a natural aptitude for, loves doing, and which help the individual to attain optimal functioning while they pursue valued ends." This wide definition allows for the inclusion of skills that are not covered by a specific classification; it does not make predictions about the results of using skills, but it does require that using skills be enjoyable. The attributes of a person that enable them to perform successfully or at their personal best, including "personal, physical, and psychological strengths," is an even broader, more current definition of "personal strengths."

The Virtues Project (TVP)

In the late 1990s, Linda Kavelin-Popov, her husband Dr. Dan Popov, and her brother John Kavelin established The Virtues Project (TVP) in Canada. The endeavor was built on the premise that virtues are the fundamental components of human goodness and that goodness is innate in all persons. The TVP offers a list of 100 virtues as well as five language-based teaching methods for cultivating each one. The TVP was created as a tool to assist parents, educators, and others in educating children morally. TVP has been used in programs for adult moral education, community group work, conflict resolution efforts, and as a tool for counsellors in more recent years. They have also been used in initiatives to aid prisoners.

Anecdotal evidence confirms the beneficial effects TVP has had on moral growth and conflict resolution over a long period of time in various countries.

A virtue ethics approach contends that moral qualities and virtues are fostered when leaders use moral speech. Inspiring, motivating, collaborating, and creating meaning are all daily practices of leadership that present possibilities for leaders to express and serve as role models for virtues. TVP techniques capitalize on the naturally communicative aspect of leadership, reflect the virtue ethics position of the significance of moral rhetoric, and overlay the daily dynamics of corporate leadership by making the assumption that language is the greatest approach to cultivate virtue.

The TVP classification includes all of the characteristics that other scholars have shown to be essential for virtuous leadership.

For instance, in their conceptualization of virtuous leadership, Rick Hackett and Gordon Wang name the six virtues of courage, temperance, justice, prudence, humanity, and truthfulness; Ronald Riggio et al. consider prudence, fortitude, temperance, and justice to be the cardinal virtues of leadership.

The 100 virtues of TVP, on the other hand, were drawn from ancient sacred writings and indigenous oral traditions that placed a greater emphasis on human flourishing than on instrumental results. This strategy is more in line with a humanities-based orientation than a social-scientific one. In keeping with a multidisciplinary approach, TVP can improve even leadership theories that aren't explicitly based on virtues.

Toby Newstead and colleagues conducted a research study published in *Leadership,* which evaluated the effectiveness of the TVP program which provided a longitudinal comparative case design over a five month period for a group of leaders. They concluded that TVP "facilitated the development of their leadership by enabling them to understand and recognize the best in themselves and others (virtues) and to incorporate virtues into their leadership practices."

Virtues of Leadership

Many theories of leadership that do not explicitly advocate a virtues-based approach yet make implicit mention of the value of virtues and how they support moral and altruistic leadership. For instance, Keith Grint's analysis of the challenges of leadership or Ronald Heifetz and Harold Linsky's study of the ethics or goodness suggested by questions pointing to higher values and possibilities to make a difference. By drawing on the work of virtue theorist Alasdair MacIntyre, several academics' examination of the purpose of leadership also alludes to the moral or ethical dimensions of leading and suggests the importance of virtues.

While not openly centered on virtues or founded in virtue ethics, these approaches to leadership can still be improved by promoting TVP as a program to cultivate virtues and hence support ethical and prosocial leadership.

A review of the literature on moral, ethical, spiritual, charismatic, transformational, and visionary leadership was carried out in 2012 by Rick Hackett and Gordon Wang. They identified 59 virtues that were conceptualized as leader character traits in these literatures as a result of their review. Others just cite virtues when describing strong leaders and leadership processes as they are according to their theory. Some leadership theories describe virtues as essential qualities.

Cultural Backgrounds of Virtues

Philosophers, spiritual authorities, and literary giants have long debated the topic of living a virtue-filled life and the virtues that should be embraced.

Christian Character

These virtues are highlighted more than any others in the Bible and other Christian literature:

- Love: love for every creature created by God.

- Honesty: keeping your promises and commitments.

- Trust: Complete dependence on the honesty, competence, or character of a person or thing.

- Kindness: good will, and beneficent behavior.

- Hope: the conviction that things can improve and difficult times will pass.

- Charity: showing compassion for other people.

- Responsibility: accepting responsibility for one's acts and life.

- Compassion: the ability to feel other people's pain and act to relieve it.

- Prudence: the capacity to control and regulate oneself rationally.

- Justice: the morally correct behavior or attitude.

- Patience: the ability to endure calmly; tolerance.

- Courage: endurance, bravery, perseverance, fearlessness .

- Respect: tolerance, deference, non-judgment.

Virtues and Meanings of Confucianism

- Courage: "Yong": assisting others in overcoming fear.

- Temperance: "Zhongyong," which emphasizes the management of emotional reactions to pleasure and suffering regardless of their causes .

- Justice: "Yi": determining if a course of action is morally good or wrong and educating people on what is morally appropriate.

- Prudence: "Zhi": relating to environment appraisal, truth identification, and decision of appropriate (or good) action.

- Humanity: "Ren": encouraging others to "do good."

- Honesty: "Xin": maintaining integrity and speaking the truth.

The Virtues of Aristotle

- Courage: conquering the fear that results from acting appropriately for the intended purpose at the appropriate moment and in the appropriate manner; a quality that enables leaders to act fearlessly in accordance with their moral principles.

- Temper: relating to the pleasure and agony brought on by one's own health, fitness, and appetite; a quality that aids leaders in maintaining emotional self-control and self-gratification needs.

- Justice: informing individuals of the proper course of action (treating others fairly); a quality that encourages the respectful awareness and defense of others' rights to fair treatment in line with standardized criteria.

- Prudence: in terms of evaluating the environment, determining the truth; and determining what is appropriate (or beneficial) to do, a quality of character that enables leaders to make the "correct" decisions and pick the "right" methods to accomplish the "right" objectives.

- Friendship: enabling others to show kindness; a quality of a leader that underlies their regard for, and affection for, others.

- Honesty: encouraging others to remain sincere and speak the truth; a quality of character exhibited by leaders who are trustworthy and dependable.

Exemplary Leadership

The relationship between virtue and leadership is demonstrated by a number of ethical and virtuous leadership ideas. For instance, C. L. Pearce and colleagues contend that moral leadership encourages shared leadership, which in turn promotes organizational learning, in their article published in the *Journal of Management, Spirituality, and Religion*. While R.E. Riggio and colleagues contend in the *Consulting Psychology Journal* that moral leaders encourage followers to feel more empowered and identify with their organizations. Similar to this, moral leaders serve as rudders to efficiently navigate change and promote instrumental outcomes connected to performance, according to K. Cameron's paper in the *Journal of Business Ethics.*

Virtuous leadership fosters peace and stability among companies, according to L. Lang and colleagues. Behaving morally, being happy, and improving performance are the three main effects that virtues have on leaders, according to Rick D. Hackett and Gordon Wang. Additionally, Ryan Fehr and colleagues propose that followers' evaluations of a leader's moral character and virtue encourage them to act in a way that is compatible with their ideals.

These theories of effective leadership accept that the development and practice of virtues are necessary for us to live together harmoniously and to work toward shared objectives, as demonstrated by Christopher Peterson and Martin Seligman in their studies. Human groups cannot thrive without values such as justice, temperance, humanity, and wisdom.

Key Questions

However, it is still unclear how we may promote virtues to create effective leaders and strong leadership habits. How do we develop our theories of moral leadership such that they can be put into action? Despite requests to improve or expand such interventions, searches of academic archives turn up very little theoretical work on explicitly virtues-based leadership development programs. There has never been a greater urgent need to put values into practice and incorporate them into organizational leadership. Despite this well-established heritage of academia, organizational research and leadership development appear to be underemphasized in our current approach.

Taya R. Cohen and Lily Morse propose a tripartite model for understanding moral character, with the premise that there are motivational, ability, and identity factors, in their study of moral character in organizations, which was published in *Research in Organizational Behavior*. They contend that consideration of others — taking into account the wants, needs, and implications of others — is an essential component of motivation. The ability component is self-regulation, or controlling one's actions and emotions in a way that has advantageous outcomes. The moral identity component of identification is the value placed on morality and the desire to see oneself as moral.

Consider hiring the very worst person. The employee could be characterized as careless, slothful, dishonest, and selfish. In other words, a perfect balancing act between high neuroticism and low conscientiousness in terms of the Big Five personality traits.

Additionally, this dreadful employee would be less inclined to feel bad about behaving selfishly and negatively. This person would regularly act in a way that is counterproductive and detrimental to the organization and the people who work there. Finally, the worst possible employee would have a low moral identity, which means that being a good person would be irrelevant to—or even in conflict with—his or her self-concept, in addition to lacking care for others and having poor self-regulation skills. Simply said, the poorest employee possesses low moral character in addition to any other undesirable traits that may exist in terms of skills and talents.

There is a growing consensus among psychologists that what is right and wrong should be conceptualized as that which regulates social relationships and facilitates group living, despite the fact that the question of "what is ethical" has been the subject of much debate and definitional ambiguity within the organizational behavior literature.

Twelve two-year projects sponsored by the John Templeton Foundation, the Psychology of Character grant competition, the Character Project at Wake Forest University, and the moral philosophers Christian Miller, William Fleeson, and Michael Furr examined the existence, nature, and connection between character and moral behavior. **According to an assessment made by the researchers at the Character Project, 20–30% of working adults in the U.S. are employees who lack moral character.**

The Connection Between Virtue and the Development of Leadership

The connection between virtue, character, and leadership is the main justification for a virtues-based approach to leadership development. *The Ethics of Leadership* author Joanne Ciulla contends that moral character is made up of virtues and that human leaders have moral character.

Although David Day and colleagues argue in their chapter in the *Sage Handbook of Leadership* that excellent leadership must go beyond simple instruction and the lessons learned early in life, leadership can also be learned and can be taught. A complicated life experience and trigger events are taken into account when good leadership develops. Both the development of virtue and the development of leadership involve ongoing education, habit formation, and improvement. Both leadership and morality are acquired early in life and require ongoing growth.

Moral Leadership

Moralized leadership refers to methods and actions taken by a leader rather than character attributes. According to the concept of "moralized leadership," a leader's actions and methods influence their followers' moral development and behavior in accordance with their principles. The theories of effective leadership, such as Wang and Hackett's notion of virtuous leadership, which focuses on six virtues as crucial leader attributes, offer a different perspective.

In their study, Ryan Fehr et al. explain how followers will moralize leader behavior that resonates with the followers' own moral orientation towards one or more moral foundations and describe leader behaviors likely to result in followers' positive moralization. Their findings were published in the journal *The Academy of Management Proceedings*. In other words, Fehr et al. argue representative behaviors are likely to be accepted as "correct" or "good" by followers. It is intended that these actions will inspire followers to adopt similar behaviors that are consistent with their ideals.

Virtues, Ethics, and Values

In his research of ethical leadership, J.B. Brown makes the case that creating virtuous leaders begins with identifying, shaping, and building one's own basic principles through time. His analysis showed that 95% of the 3,257 executives and workers who established their core values through facilitation and coaching from 2002 to 2009 chose integrity as the most significant virtue. Behavioral indicators including honesty, truth, ethics, justice, and doing the right thing were among the most constant, despite modest variations in how they characterized it. When contrasted to their current conduct, many people found that developing their personal core principles and increasing their ethical awareness had a profound impact on their lives.

Before anyone rushes out and decides to start the process of creating morally upright leaders within their firm, remember that there is a serious warning to heed, advises Brown. People are virtually always drawn to and wish to imitate virtuous ethical leadership when they first begin to examine what that looks like. Unintentionally, this understanding causes individuals to quickly learn what immoral, self-centered leadership looks like and to despise it. Followers, especially those with awareness of what constitutes a virtuous and ethical leader, disengage and/or depart in disgust when executives and managers talk the talk but don't walk the walk.

Brown suggests the following as components of virtuous leadership development:

1. Create an organization-wide shared vision, mission, and values. This sets the bar for behavior for all organization stakeholders and directs the organization in the direction that its leadership wants it to go. Applying an understanding of applied ethics, use a facilitation/coaching method to help the CEO and a small senior team (to help hold the CEO accountable):

   • What are ethics and making ethical decisions?

   • Why practice ethics? - Benefits and difficulties

   • The most common rationalizations and justifications for unethical activity (e.g., "I was following orders," or "everyone else does it."

2. Create a prescriptive procedure for making ethical decisions that takes into account: The advantages and disadvantages of consequentialist, deontological, and virtuous/integrity applications (most people tend to filter right decisions from one of these applications). The trick is to be able to weigh the benefits and drawbacks of each and decide which application is most appropriate in a specific circumstance (ethics unlike morality, is grey, not black and white).

3. Create a decision-making matrix with ethical filters that will help you use consequentialist, deontological, and virtuous/integrity applications to help you come to the best conclusion.

   - Create corporate core values that cover morality.

   - Create a compliance structure that includes whistleblower protections for unethical, immoral, and values-violating activity.

   - Add the golden rule to your company's core values and compliance procedures.

   - Create a method to help each employee in the organization discover and communicate their personal value system.

   - Include moral and virtue-based conduct components in performance evaluation systems.

Aligning The Values Project (TVP) to Leadership Theory

TVP techniques promote and foster the virtue of both the doer (a leader) and the done to (a leader's counterpart), or the internal inclination toward good. It is impossible to foresee, nevertheless, which virtues people would prioritize cultivating. For instance, a leader at organization A would want to foster greater creativity, so he or she might use Speak the Language of Virtues to express inventiveness when observing a subordinate doing something new. While working in company B, a leader may be trying to instill courage in the workforce and may Speak the Language of Virtues to express gratitude when they see an employee displaying courage. Similar actions could be seen as chances to appreciate and cultivate various virtues. Therefore, the leaders should determine the intended consequences when certain qualities are displayed rather than suggesting which tactics will create what virtues.

Adopting a leader-centric perspective does not imply that influence flows in a single route from leader to follower. Furthermore, it does not suggest that leaders and followers are "two kinds of individuals" with unique differences. The emphasis on leaders reflects the widely held belief that those in positions of authority exercise proportionately more influence and power within organizations. The emphasis on leaders also acknowledges the role of leaders as gatekeepers and influencers inside organizations. By focusing development interventions, like TVP, on leaders, we have the chance to change the entire corporate culture.

A departure from the disagreements over a single definition of leadership and the profusion of descriptive leadership theories is represented by the virtues-based approach to leadership development. Joanna Ciulla explains, "We are not unclear about what leaders do, but we would like to know the best way to do it. Virtue is the tendency we have as humans to think, feel, and act in ways that are morally excellent and advance the common good, and leadership is the human activity of inspiring others to take an action. We can help leaders be and do good by adopting a virtues-based leadership development perspective and using tools like the TVP."

Final Thoughts and Questions to Consider

There's an overlap between character strengths, values and virtues and there also can be nuances and situational differences. For example, a character strength and virtue can be honesty. Contextually this can show up as "walk your talk" or "be good for your word" behavior which is a character strength, whereas the virtue of being honest can be applied to all situations and is also a value.

Here are some questions to consider:

1. What virtues are the most important to you?

2. In what situations or contexts do those virtues appear?

3. Are your top virtues also your top values ?

Chapter 5

Moral and Ethical Leadership

"Ethics is knowing the difference between what you have the right to do and what is right to do."

— Judge Potter Stewart

O xford Dictionaries defines ethics as "Moral principles that govern a person's behavior or the conducting of an activity."

The problem is that not all people adhere to the same moral standards in today's society. Some are common to everyone. For instance, killing and stealing are morally wrong, but attitudes on other topics, such as the ethics of animal research or abortion, varying according to religion, culture, personal beliefs, politics and laws.

Sometimes a moral or ethical principle comes into conflict with another moral or ethical principle. An example is the issue of freedom of speech. What if one of your employees exercises that freedom but the language is abusive to another employee or the boss.

So ethical leadership means staying true to your moral principles, while also being aware of the complexity of some ethical issues and being sensitive to the differing views of your employees and managing the conflicts that may arise.

Unfortunately, ethics and leadership don't always go together. According to a study by the *Institute of Leadership & Management*:

- 63% of managers have been asked to do something contrary to their own ethical code.

- 43% have been told to behave in direct violation of their organization's own values statements.

- 19% have been asked to break the law.

The Benefits of Ethical Leadership

When the post mortems were conducted on various corporate and political scandals over the years, it became clear that the mistakes could have been avoided if strong ethical leadership had was present and managers had prevented the wrongdoing before it escalated.

Studies have found practical, positive benefits as well. For example, one study at Cornell University concluded "ethical leadership was positively and significantly related to employee performance."

Another study published in *Science Direct* revealed that ethical leadership reduced employee turnover, a significant benefit given the high cost of employee turnover.

Although academics have long debated the subject of ethical leadership, descriptive research on what ethical leadership entails is relatively new. Some of the first studies focused on defining ethical leadership was by Linda K. Treviñob and colleagues. Their research revealed that ethical leaders could be described along two dimensions: moral person and moral manager.

According to the researchers, the moral person dimension refers to the qualities of the ethical leader as a person. Strong moral persons are honest and trustworthy. They demonstrate a concern for other people. They are also seen as approachable. Employees approach these moral persons with problems and concerns, knowing that they will be "heard and seen." Moral persons have a reputation for being fair and principled and act consistently on those principles. Lastly, moral persons are seen as consistently moral in both their personal and professional lives, rather than having two different lives.

The moral manager refers to how the leader uses the position of leadership to promote ethical conduct at work. Strong moral managers act as role models in the workplace. They make ethics real by modeling ethical conduct to their employees. Moral managers establish and communicate ethical standards using rewards and punishments to ensure those standards are followed. In sum, leaders who are moral managers "walk the talk" *and* "talk the walk".

People who try to appear to be strong moral managers who are weak moral persons are likely to be seen as hypocrites, failing to practice what they preach. Hypocritical leaders often talk about the importance of ethics, but their actions can be unethical and amoral. Conversely, a strong moral person in their personal lives who is a weak moral manager runs the risk of being seen as an ethically "neutral" leader, being silent on ethical work issues, suggesting to employees that the leader is not concerned about ethics.

Unethical Behavior Can Spread Among Employees

Recent research shows that ethical leadership is related to important follower outcomes, such as employees' job satisfaction, organizational commitment, willingness to report problems to supervisors, industriousness, are focal about standards and perceptions of organizational culture and ethical climate. At the group level, ethical leadership is positively related to organizational citizenship behavior and psychological safety, and negatively related to workplace deviance.

Traditional leadership literature has not described destructive leader behavior as "unethical"; however, the implication is clear. Unethical behavior involves acts that are contrary to an organizations ethical rules, and is illegal and/or are morally inappropriate to larger society. Research into behaviors of leaders with "dark triad" characteristics has uncovered a variety of unethical leader acts. Various terms have evolved in the literature, such as abusive supervision, supervisor toxic leadership, and tyrannical leadership. Research shows these leaders are manipulative, abusive, and toxic. Their actions are perceived as intentionally harmful, and may be the source of legal action against employers. Therefore, by these measures, destructive leader behavior is unethical.

Unethical leadership transcends beyond the leaders' own behavior. In seeking to accomplish organizational goals, leaders can encourage corrupt and unethical acts within their organizations. For instance, a review of corporate scandals in *Fortune 100* corporations concluded that actions perpetrated by executives, boards of directors, and government officials were the primary cause of such transgressions.

Leaders can foster unethical behavior among followers without engaging in the behavior themselves and do so by way of rewards, condoning non-conformers, and ignoring unethical acts. Qualitative research shows leaders who reward short-term results, model aggressive and Machiavellian behavior, do not punish followers' wrongdoing, end up promoting like-minded individuals, and heighten unethical behavior within organizations. Also, research shows employees who engage in unethical acts to boost organizational performance or help the organization in some other way help to spread unethical practices. Such embedded practices in an organization can protect leaders from primary blame, essentially providing them "plausible deniability".

One of the most common and reprehensible defenses that unethical followers use when engaging in unethical (and/or immoral) behavior is that they were just "following orders" given by the leader(s).

The influence of what many have described as an unethical, narcissistic sociopath like Donald Trump cannot be underestimated. During his presidency he has given the green light to thousands of leaders and followers throughout the country to act in unethical, amoral and immoral ways. "If the person at the top can do it, then it's okay for me too," many of them would argue.

The Lack of Self-Regulation

Self-regulation principles of behavior have also been used to explain why unethical leadership occurs. In particular, this explanation draws from the social cognitive theory of moral thought and action which suggests that leaders may behave unethically because they disconnect themselves from moral standards and rationalize unethical treatment toward their employees. For example, researchers Marie S. Mitchell and her colleagues found in their study published in the *Journal of Applied*

Psychology that leaders who were engaged in abusive behaviors thought doing so was justified against employees who were critical of the leader.

Researchers Leanne S. Son Hing, and her colleagues published a study in the *Journal of Personality and Social Psychology* that showed leaders with a strong social dominance orientation were more likely to engage in unethical behavior, particularly when followers were more agreeable; and/ or followers high in conservative authoritarianism, as evidenced more frequently with Republicans than with Democrats.

There is a clear connection between emotions and ethical judgment. Emotions inform us when things are not right, and act as ethical alarms. Rommel Salvador and Robert Folger highlight this point in their study in the *Business Ethics Review* and discuss the role of emotions on ethical judgments with the human brain. Their review suggests "emotions consciously and unconsciously influence ethical decision making and behavior."

Emotional contagion is defined as "an unconscious transfer of emotion, which fosters mimicry of another's emotional state." Research shows employees who perceive their leaders displaying more positive than negative emotions experience more positive and less negative moods themselves. This is known as a viral effect. The authors argue groups with leaders who display positive emotions exhibit more coordination and expend less effort than groups with negatively affective leaders. Additionally, positive emotional displays from leaders influence followers' perceptions of their leader (e.g., effectiveness, motivational ability) and important outcomes, such as citizenship behavior and performance.

Leaders can elicit negative emotions among their followers and they are often more intense than positive emotions. Negative emotional reactions to leaders can spread throughout an organization as emotional contagion, ultimately hurting the group's climate and heightening cynicism about the leader.

Emotional, attitudinal, and behavioral reactions to leaders' emotions have been generally explained by affective events theory and emotional transference principles. Leaders can control and shape events within organizations and these events "transfer" the emotional state of followers. The result can be impulsive and destructive behavior. Over time, long-term attitudes can be affected. The influence of negative emotions can be even more impactful because negative emotions are felt with greater intensity compared to positive emotions.

Additionally, research shows that we expect ethical leadership will trigger more positive follower emotions (e.g., gratitude, awe, enthusiasm, empathy), whereas unethical leadership should affect more negative emotions (e.g., anger, fear, jealousy, selfishness). The relationship between unethical leadership and follower unethical behavior would be moderated by the level of emotional contagion experienced and harnessed by the leader.

Further, research suggests the type and strength of the emotions evoked by followers will differentially influence their behavior. For instance, an employee, angered by a leader's unethical may lead the employee to retaliate with their own unethical acts (e.g.: sabotage) whereas an employee who was experiencing positive emotions such as gratitude or compassion may influence other employees to engage in ethical behavior (e.g., volunteerism, prosocial behavior).

Research shows that leaders' values have been shown to uniquely shape the organization's culture. Leaders embed their values into the framework of organizations by surrounding themselves with individuals who share their values.

Katarina Katja Mihelič and her colleagues, in their published research in the *International Journal of Management & Information Systems* on ethical leadership argue "ethical leadership can be viewed in terms of healing and energizing powers of love, recognizing that leadership is a reciprocal relation with followers. The leader's mission is to serve and support and his passion for leading comes from compassion."

To be able to influence followers' ethical behavior, the authors contend, leaders must communicate ethical standards and continually evaluate real examples. This means that focusing one-time efforts of writing a code of ethics or ethics policy **is not an adequate step** towards implementation of ethical behavior in organizations. Ethics should be the life blood of organizational life. Ethical leaders are perceived as people who do not tolerate ethical lapses, they rather hold people accountable for discipline people for unethical behavior.

A leader's character influences his ethical performance; a strong character plays an important role in effective self-leadership and in the process of leading others. D.G. Zauderer described the differences in ethical and unethical leadership, his article in *Business Forum*, as shown in this chart.

Ethical and Unethical leadership (Zauderer, 1992)

The Ethical Leader	The Unethical Leader
Is humble	Is arrogant and self-serving
Is concerned for the greater good	Excessively promotes self-interest
Is honest and straightforward	Practices deception
Honors commitments	Breaches agreements
Strives for fairness	Deals unfairly
Takes responsibility	Shifts blames to others
Show respect for each person	Diminishes others' dignity
Encourages and develops others	Neglects follower development
Serves others	Withholds help and support
Shows courage to stand up for what is right	Lacks courage to confront unjust acts

The traits that are most often attributed to good are honesty, trustworthiness and integrity. Trust is linked to credibility, consistency and predictability in relationships and honesty is essential in a trust-based relationship.

For more than a decade, leadership experts James Kouzes and Barry Posner have been asking employees around the world what they most value or want from a leader and what would it take for them to follow him willingly?

Without exception honesty is the first on the list. How is honesty determined? They observe the behavior and the consistency of behavior in a variety of situations. If a leader constantly changes his behavior, followers perceive the leader as unworthy of trust. Another thing that undermines trust is if a leader espouses one set of values (the way he should behave) and actively promotes them, whereas personally practices another set, usually out of self-interest.

Harvard Business School Professor Joseph L. Baradarcco believes that a leader needs to embrace a more complex code of ethical behavior compared to the one learned in childhood and adolescence. He contends that real morality is not binary but rather emerges in many shades of gray. This is why leaders need ethical codes that are not simplistic. Consequently, leaders need to embrace a wider set of human values and constantly evaluate their own basic personal values.

Max Bazerman, the author of *Better, Not Perfect: A Realist's Guide to Maximum Sustainable Goodness*, and an article in the *Harvard Business Review*, "A New Model for Ethical Leadership," argues that leaders "should be guided by the goal of creating the most value for society. Moving beyond a set of simple ethical rules ('Don't lie,' 'Don't cheat'), this perspective—rooted in the work of the philosophers Jeremy Bentham, John Stuart Mill, and Peter Singer—provides the clarity needed to make a wide variety of important managerial decisions."

Bazerman's perspective is essentially utilitarian: "maximizing aggregate well-being and minimizing aggregate pain, goals that are helped by pursuing efficiency in decision-making, reaching moral decisions without regard for self-interest, and avoiding tribal behavior (such as nationalism or in-group favoritism)." Or in other words, the greatest good for the greatest number.

Bazerman argues that far too many executives consciously or unconsciously overlook unethical behavior if it benefits them or the company. Bazerman says that the concept of "bounded rationality," sees managers as wanting to be rational but end up being influenced by their biases.

He argues that we struggle with systematic cognitive (bias) barriers that prevent us from being as ethical as we want to be. By adjusting our personal goals from serving self-interest and that of the organization to behaving as ethically as possible for the benefit of society and the planet we can establish a sort of North Star to guide us.

Daniel Kahneman's book *Thinking, Fast and Slow* know, describes how we have two very different modes of decision-making:

- System 1 is our intuitive system, or our gut instinct, which is fast, automatic, effortless, and emotional. Kahneman says System 1 is used to make most decisions.

- System 2 is our deliberative rational and logical thinking, which is slower, conscious and takes effort. Kahneman argues that System 2 leads to more ethical behaviors.

Intuition gut instinct and emotions tend to dominate decision-making Bazerman says. When evaluating one option (such as a single job offer or a single potential charitable contribution), we lean on System 1 processing, he argues. But when we have to consider multiple choices, our decisions tend to be more carefully considered and less biased. For example, we may donate to charity on the basis of emotional tugs when we consider charities in isolation; but when we compare several charities, we tend to think more about where our contribution will do the greatest good, which is a utilitarian choice.

Similarly, research published *in HKS Working Paper* by the economists Iris Bohnet and Alexandra van Geen, found that when people evaluate job candidates one at a time, System 1 is activated, and they tend to fall back on gender stereotypes. For example, interviewers are more likely to hire men for mathematical tasks. But when they compare two or more applicants at a time, preferably without being influenced by physical appearance, they focus more on job-relevant criteria, are more ethical (less sexist), hire better candidates, and obtain better results for the organization.

Another decision-making strategy involves adapting what the philosopher John Rawls called the *veil of ignorance*. Rawls argued that if you thought about how society should be structured without knowing your status in it (rich or poor, man or woman, black or white)—that is, behind a veil of ignorance—you would make fairer, more-ethical decisions. Indeed, recent empirical research published in the *Proceedings of the National Academy of Sciences* by Karen Huang and Joshua Greene shows that those who make ethical decisions behind a veil of ignorance do create more value.

Bazerman observes, "Whatever your organization, I'm guessing it's quite socially responsible in some ways but less so in others, and you may be uncomfortable with the latter. Most organizations get higher ethical marks on some dimensions than on others. I know companies whose products make the world worse, but they have good diversity and inclusion policies. I know others whose products make the world better, but they engage in unfair competition that destroys value in their business ecosystem. Most of us are ethically inconsistent as well. Otherwise honest people may view deception in negotiation with a client or a colleague as completely acceptable. If we care about the value or harm we create, remembering that we're likely to be ethical in some domains and unethical in others can help us identify where change might be most useful."

Bazerman uses the example of Andrew Carnegie, who donated $350 million, or 90% of his wealth, to fund more than 2,500 libraries as well as Carnegie Hall and the Carnegie Foundation. He was not, however, only a good man of charity. As a corporate executive, he also displayed miserly, ineffective, and perhaps illegal actions, such as forcefully eliminating the union at his steel factory in Homestead, Pennsylvania.

According to Bazerman, the Sackler family, who hold the enormous pharmaceutical company Purdue Pharma, have demonstrated this difference between right and wrong behavior. With money produced from the family company, the Sacklers have made large grants to museums, scientific research centers, and universities, including

Harvard. But by aggressively selling the addictive pain killer OxyContin, Purdue Pharma made billions. More than 15,000 Americans had died as a result of OxyContin by 2018, and the drug has since become a major public health issue. The Sacklers have also accepted little personal accountability, despite the fact that the corporation has made some restitution yet OxyContin has increased their personal fortune.

Bazerman contends that leaders are capable of far more than simply improving their own conduct. They can significantly increase the amount of good they accomplish by inspiring others to do better since they are accountable for both the actions of others and their own.

By influencing the context in which others make decisions, leaders can also add more value and behave more morally. Richard Thaler and Cass Sunstein explain how we may shape the "infrastructure" surrounding options to influence people to make value-creating choices in their book Nudge. The most frequent kind of nudge may include altering the default option that decision-makers are presented with. In some European countries, a well-known nudge promotes organ donation by automatically registering residents in the program and allowing them to opt out if they so choose. With the help of the program, the percentage of people who agreed to be donors rose from less than 30% to more than 80%.

According to Bazerman, "new ethical dilemmas confront us every day, ranging from how to allocate limited medical supplies during a pandemic to what algorithm to build for self-driving cars. As technology develops incredible methods to enhance our lives, our environmental impact becoming more important. When their leaders reject System 2 thinking and even truth itself, many nations struggle with what to do. Finding shared value also no longer serves as a national objective in far too many nations. We all want our leaders to lead in an ethical manner.

Throughout America's history we've seen other examples of a lack of ethical behavior or conflict in values. For example, one of founders of the American Republic, Thomas Jefferson wrote that "all men are created equal," in the Declaration of Independence and yet enslaved more than 600 people over the course of his life. George Washington, America's first president, was a slave owner. The year 1780 saw Pennsylvania pass the General Abolition Act, which automatically freed enslaved people who lived in the state for half a year, along with any enslaved person over the age of 28. Washington's solution to losing his slaves was to rotate their service. He would send them back to his estate, Mount Vernon in Virginia, every six months, just before they were due to earn their freedom. When the slaves returned to Pennsylvania, the six month timer reset and Washington could continue to keep them as property.

Bazerman argues that leaders can do far more than just make their own behavior more ethical. Because they are responsible for the decisions of others as well as their own, they can dramatically multiply the amount of good they do by encouraging others to be better.

Leaders can also create more value and act more ethically by shaping the environment in which others make decisions. In their book *Nudge*, Richard Thaler and Cass Sunstein describe how we can design the "architecture" surrounding choices to prompt people to make value-creating decisions. Perhaps the most common type of nudge involves changing the default choice that decision-makers face. A famous nudge encourages organ donation in some European nations by enrolling citizens in the system automatically, letting them opt out if they wish. The program increased the proportion of people agreeing to be donors from less than 30% to more than 80%.

Bazerman contends that "new ethical challenges confront us daily, from what algorithm to create for self-driving cars to how to allocate scarce medical supplies during a pandemic. As technology creates amazing ways to improve our lives, our environmental footprint becomes a bigger concern. Many countries struggle with how to act when their leaders reject System 2 thinking and even truth itself. And in too many countries, finding collective value is no longer a national goal. We all crave ethical direction from our leaders."

Assessing Leaders Ethics

Several scholars support the need to go beyond standard personality assessments in order to better understand how behavior is shaped (Hogan & Kaiser, 2005; Judge, Piccolo, & Kosalka, 2009), and there are a number of instruments that exist across a variety of disciplines that may provide the basis for a framework to assess and measure several key components of ethical leadership and can be used to measure subordinates' perspectives on supervisor ethical behavior. These include, and could be used as part of the Assessment phase of the ACS model:

- Perceived Leader Integrity Scale (PLIS), (Craig & Gustafson, 1998) – measures follower perception of leader's trustworthiness, civility, self-centeredness, honesty and evil.

- The Ethical Leadership Scale (ELS) (Brown et al., 2005) – measures follower perception of leader's fairness, trustworthiness, doing right thing, reward and punishment.

- Leadership Virtues Questionnaire (LVQ), (Riggio, Zhu & Reina, 2010) – measures follower perception of leader's prudence, fortitude, temperance and justice.

- The Ethical Leadership at Work Scale (ELWS) (Kalshoven, Den Hartog, & De Hoogh, 2011) – measures follower perception of leader's fairness, integrity, ethical guidance, people orientation, power sharing, role clarification and concern for sustainability.

- The Ethical Leadership Questionnaire (ELQ) (Yukl, Mahsud, Hassan, & Prussia, 2013) – measures follower perception of leader's honesty, fairness, setting examples and concern for values.

Final Thoughts and Questions to Consider

Both morality and ethics loosely have to do with distinguishing the difference between "good and bad" or "right and wrong." Many people think of morality as something that's personal and normative, whereas ethics is the standards of "good and bad" distinguished by a certain community or social setting. We tend to think of morality as principles or rules we would follow in any context or situation, whereas ethics usually refers to rules of behavior in an organization or institution.

Here are some questions to consider:

1. Why do you consider yourself a "moral person?"

2. What moral principles or rules do you hold to be the most important?

3. What ethical standards, policies and rules should govern an organization? How would you put that in place and enforce it?

Chapter 6

Ethical Organizations and Virtuous Leaders of Good Character

"In looking for people to hire, look for three qualities: Integrity, intelligence and energy. And if they don't have the first, the other two will kill you."

— Warren Buffett

There are many shining examples of great corporate cultures and exceptional leaders of strong character—even though I've given extensive examples of the absence of ethics in firms and leaders of weak character and missing virtues.

The Ethical Organizations

The Green Citizen produces a list of the most ethical corporations in the world. This socially conscious company is driven to offer everyone useful information and services so that everyone can live sustainably. Aflac, Ecolab, International Paper, PepsiCo, Accenture, and Cummins were among the 22 businesses listed in 2022. These businesses support honest and moral business conduct, employ environmentally friendly materials, and are conscious of their social responsibility. While doing no damage reduces risks for some brands, other businesses have grasped the enormous potential of business ethics.

The World's Most Ethical Companies are Announced by Ethisphere in 2021. The 15th annual honoring of businesses that have shown a dedication to moral business conduct through initiatives that have a good influence on staff, communities, and other stakeholders, as well as on sustainable and successful long-term corporate performance.

"The endeavors and deeds of the honorees of the World's Most Ethical Companies continue to inspire us. Business, more than any other institution, was most trusted during the difficult times of 2020 because of the leadership of this group of enterprises, according to Timothy Erblich, CEO of Ethisphere. "Honorees combine company strategy with ethics and values. They take initiative, speak out, behave honestly, and look for novel methods to change the world. We acknowledge their efforts."

The publicly traded firms recognized as the World's Most Ethical Companies, as measured by Ethisphere's 2021 Ethics Index, outperformed a comparable index of big size companies by 7.1 percentage points over the previous five calendar years.

The World's Most Ethical Companies assessment process, which is based on Ethisphere's unique Ethics Quotient, considers more than 200 data points related to culture, environmental and social practices, ethics and compliance activities, governance, diversity, and initiatives to support a robust value chain. The procedure acts as a framework for capturing and codifying the best practices used by businesses globally and across all industries. The top 13 most moral businesses to work for include Aflac, International Paper, PepsiCo, Deere & Company, and Xerox.

10 Excellent Business Cases of Ethical Decision-Making

- **The choice made by Costco to pay fair wages.** Costco's success is largely attributed to the excellent customer service provided by contented workers. The fact that Costco is ready to pay higher than average compensation is one factor in its ability to draw in top talent. Because it can entice the best employees, Costco thrives. Costco also avoids labor disputes, high employee turnover, and conflict since its staff is content.

- **Volkswagen's Plan for Staff Reduction Without Layoffs.** Volkswagen AG (GR: VOW) adheres to a traditional German practice by cutting its employment without laying off any employees. To put it simply, Volkswagen reduces employment by failing to fill open positions. For instance, Volkswagen doesn't bring on new employees to replace departing employees. Avoiding layoffs is a wise idea since it boosts employee morale.

- **Best Buy's Sustainability Commitment.** In February 2019, Barron's dubbed Best Buy (NYSE: BBY), a retailer of electronics, "America's most sustainable corporation." Hubert Joly, the CEO of Best Buy, is dedicated to minimizing the environmental effect of his business through waste reduction. Additionally, Best Buy runs Teen Tech Centers where underprivileged young Americans are taught the fundamentals of technology. Teen Tech Centers aid Best Buy in expanding its workforce by producing qualified workers, according to Retail Dive. Teen Tech Centers also assist in lowering unemployment in America, where there is a severe lack of vocational education. The success of a business depends on making moral decisions, as demonstrated by Best Buy. This

113

business' dedication to morality and customer care is enabling it to endure America's retail apocalypse.

- **Chick-fil-A covers employee training costs.** The American fast food company will provide employees with up to $25,000 in tuition help. Additionally, according to Restaurant Business, Chick-fil-A claims to have paid 53,000 employees $75 million in tuition.

- **Tom's Shoes participates in charitable activities.** More than 60 million(!) pairs of shoes have been given away by the TOMS shoe company to children in need worldwide since 2006. In addition, TOMS' eyewear branch has donated more than 400,000 pairs of glasses to people who are blind and cannot afford ophthalmological care. Through its coffee business, the company has expanded its activities to include clean water efforts, and its bag line has supported programs to increase access to birthing kits for expectant mothers in poor countries as well as training for birth attendants. Over 25,000 women have received safe childbirth assistance from TOMS to this point.

- **Hootsuite, a social media management tool established in Vancouver.** Over 16 million users and 1500 staff utilize Hootsuite. The goal of Hootsuite is to have an effect and make a significant contribution. They are committed to funding opportunities for learning and skill development in order to invest in the experience and advancement of their personnel. Hootsuite has even put in place a stretch program that enables high performers to try out several jobs and find the one that fits them best. Hootsuite registered as a B-Corp in 2015, joining a group of companies that place a high value on equity, diversity, sustainability, and inclusion.

- **Canadian eCommerce behemoth Shopify.** The omnichannel commerce platform Shopify, which supports over 1 million merchants globally, has all the tools you need to launch and manage an online business. Permanent, full-time employees receive a self-directed allowance that they can use for their health and wellness or a charity giving account in addition to a complete benefits package. Being a moral leader counts, according to a survey done by LRN Corporation, a corporate ethics and compliance agency. According to the survey's total respondents, 83 percent think that if the Golden Rule were followed, their organizations would probably make better judgments, and 59 percent think that their businesses may be more successful if their executives had greater moral authority.

Ethical and Good Character Leaders

During a panel discussion with three prominent CEOs from top companies, including Ms. Lundgren, Roger Krone of Leidos, and Jonas Prising of Manpower Group, it was stated by Tamara Lundgren, President and Chief Executive Officer, Schnitzer Steel Industries, Inc., that "we are not born with character, it's not inherent, it's something we have control over." The discussion was moderated by Liban Jama, Partner/Principal, EY's We concentrate on the "variables we can control, one of which is character because there are numerous factors outside our control."

CEO of Sodexo Corporate Services Worldwide, Sylvia Metayer. She is the head of Sodexo's Corporate Services division, which leads the globe in enhancing the quality of life for 75 million people. She is French-British-Canadian. Sodexo was listed as one of Fortune's "World's Most Admired Companies" in 2016 for the fifth consecutive year. working under her direction to comprehend what makes people successful at work. Their extensive 2017 Global Workforce Trends report serves as proof of this. They discovered six aspects of quality of life that Sodexo's services directly affect through their research.

In the Top CEOs 2021 Employees' Choice from Glassdoor, executives from Mackenzie Investments, Laurentian Bank, and Marshalls claimed the top three positions. The awards are based on the opinions of staff members who submit anonymous comments by completing a corporate review regarding the leadership of their CEO, as well as insights into their position, work environment, and employer throughout the previous year.

"Unprecedented difficulties supporting employees amid the COVID-19 issue presented themselves to business leaders all around the world during the past year. Now that the workers have spoken, it is evident that these CEOs succeeded and devised inventive ways to assist their people as the workplace underwent a radical transformation "said Glassdoor CEO Christian Sutherland-Wong. "It's encouraging to see Top CEOs who, according to their staff, responded to change, reinvented visions, and led with transparency while putting the health and safety of people first throughout a hard year."

McKenzie Investments boasts "excellent work-life balance" and "According to employee survey results on Glassdoor, the company has "wonderful people," a "strategic HR staff who understand the business," and a "fantastic culture."

With a 100% approval rating on Glassdoor, Rania Llewellyn of Laurentian Bank came in second. The organization has "a terrific team to work with," according to employees, and "leaders that are forward thinking and are responsive to input." Also included is a ""Great work-life balance" and "a welcoming environment."

According to a recent study, having excellent morals also benefits your career. The study, which was carried out by leadership consulting firm KRW International, discovered a connection between an organization's performance and the CEO's integrity. Businesses with a top leader whose moral values were highly evaluated by the workforce outperformed those with a lower character rating. Ten leaders who excelled in every area were singled out in the study. CEO of KRW International Kiel refers to these rock star executives as "virtuoso CEOs," and they include Charles Sorenson, CEO and president of Intermountain Healthcare, Sally Jewell, former CEO of outdoor store REI, and Dale Larson, CEO and president of Larson Manufacturing Company. They were viewed as speaking out for the proper causes, showing concern for others, empathetic behavior, and overcoming mistakes.

A panel at the meeting of the Business and Organizational Ethics Partnership, a program of the Markkula Center for Applied Ethics, focused on the role of the CEO in establishing a company's ethical culture.

Russell Howard, the CEO of Maxygen, Keith Krach, the former CEO of Ariba, and Tony Ridder, the CEO of Knight Ridder, all represented three quite distinct organizational perspectives. Even though they all agreed that the ethical tone is set at the top, they each had their unique strategy for fostering high ethical standards throughout their firms.

The top 20 managers at each publication are required to sign an ethics code each year, according to Ridder, the head of the second-largest newspaper group in the US. Conflicts of interest, self-dealing, gifts, and outside work are all covered by the code. It forbids making political contributions, serving on boards of for-profit businesses, and using private information for one's own gain.

As a publisher of newspapers, Knight Ridder also maintains a thorough code of ethics for all of its reporters. Additionally, it establishes a zero-tolerance policy for plagiarism and sexual harassment and prohibits political contributions.

According to Krach, the problem at Ariba was to spread the company's values while the software manufacturer grew at a pace of 100% each quarter for the first two to three years, and subsequently at a rate of 25 to 50% after that. Krach started off with what he refers to as his "playbook," which is a step-by-step manual for the organization's vision, mission, values, team rules, and goals.

Every new Maxygen employee meets for lunch with Howard, the CEO of a 200-person biotech company, where they talk about the company's ideals among other things. However, Howard also expressed skepticism about the ability of any corporate procedure to "take a rascal and make him into an ethical person." He claimed that integrity is the result of a gene-environment interaction that develops long before an employee joins Maxygen. The key, in his opinion, is finding candidates who match the company's principles of "honesty and believing passionately in what you do."

Fortune magazine ranked Johnson and Johnson's late CEO James Burke as one of the top CEOs of all time. He received plaudits for his moral leadership throughout his tenure as Johnson and Johnson's CEO. His management style was particularly apparent in 1982 when Johnson and Johnson was dealing with a Tylenol issue. The company's best-selling item at the time was Tylenol. Burke therefore had to move quickly when seven individuals in Chicago died in 1982 after eating Extra-Strength Tylenol capsules laced with cyanide. Despite the financial loss, he recalled all Tylenol items. In addition, he appeared on television to announce additional measures the business would take to safeguard its products. He even permitted the media to record company meetings where solutions to this problem were discussed. Instead of passing on the expenses to the customer, the corporation paid for all of the expenditures associated with these activities.

Tony Hsieh, a former CEO of Zappos, approaches corporate culture in an innovative and passionate manner. His strategy assisted him in developing a culture at Zappos that earned the business a spot on Fortune magazine's 2014 list of the 100 Best Companies to Work For. He was successful in incorporating ethics into Zappos' basic beliefs, which is largely responsible for his success. He anticipates that the organization's values and vision will be in harmony.

The charismatic co-founder and long-time CEO of Southwest Airlines, Herb Kelleher, built a degree of trust with his staff members and between management and the airline's unions that is unheard of in the business. Regarded as a "Moral Leader" because he was able to employ the Three P's (Principle, Purpose, and People) as his guiding ethical principles for managing the day-to-day operations of the company, Warren Buffett is an ethical leader.

Final Thoughts and Questions to Consider

There are some exemplary organizations and leaders who have set a high standard for ethics and morality.

Here are Some Questions to Consider

1. If you were to be responsible for developing a code of ethics for your organization what would you include?

2. What are some ethical organizations and leaders you admire? Why?

3. How would you encourage and train employees to follow an organizations code of ethics?

4. How would you enforce the code of ethics? What might be consequences for violation?

Chapter 7

Servant Leadership

"The servant leader is servant first. It begins with the natural feeling that one wants to serve."

— Robert K. Greenleaf

Many organizations are moving away from the conventional hierarchical, authoritarian, and autocratic organizational structures and leadership systems and toward more democratic ones that place the needs of the group above the individual. Servant leaders involve others in decision-making and place a high value on morality and virtue.

Although the concept of servant leadership dates back to antiquity, Robert K. Greenleaf, a former AT&T executive, originated the term in his pamphlet *The Servant as Leader*, an essay that was first published in 1970. "The servant-leader is servant first," Greenleaf stated, "It starts with the instinctive desire to serve first and foremost. The desire to lead is then brought about by conscious choice. That person is noticeably different from one who takes the role of leader first, perhaps due to the need to quell an odd power need or acquire monetary goods. The extreme types are the leader-first and the servant-first."

The distinction is shown in the care the servant takes to ensure that other people's highest priority requirements are met, Greenleaf continues. The most important—and challenging to administer—test is:

Did leaders help others to develop as people? Do those people who have servant leaders improve in health, wisdom, freedom, independence, and likelihood to serve others? What impact does this have on society's underprivileged groups? Will they gain something, or at least not become worse off?

Greenleaf's idea of servant leadership set off a subtle revolution in the way that we think about and approach leadership. Since the idea of servant leadership is becoming more and more recognized as the ideal leadership style to which countless individuals and businesses aspire.

The list of influential leaders and proponents of servant leadership is extensive and includes names like James Autry, Warren Bennis, Peter Block, John Carver, Stephen Covey, Max DePree, Joseph Jaworski, James Kouzes, Larraine Matusak, Parker Palmer, M. Scott Peck, Peter Senge, Peter Vaill, Margaret Wheatley, and Danah Zohar, to name just a few. *Rewiring the Corporate Brain*, Zohar's groundbreaking work on quantum sciences and leadership, states explicitly that "servant-leadership is the essence of quantum thinking and quantum leadership."

Servant Leaders Traits

1. **Listening.** Although effective communication skills are crucial for the servant leader, they must be strengthened by a strong commitment to paying close attention to what others have to say.

2. **Empathy.** Servant leaders make an effort to comprehend others' emotional states and to show compassion for them.

122

3. **Healing.** This entails mending one's relationships with others as well as oneself.

4. **Awareness.** This means awareness of one's surroundings, oneself, and the opinions and values of others.

5. **Stewardship.** Stewardship, according to Peter Block, author of *The Empowered Manager and Stewardship,* is "keeping something in trust for another." According to Robert Greenleaf, all institutions should be held in trust for the benefit of society, and CEOs, staff members, and trustees all have important responsibilities to play in this.

6. **A Dedication to Human Development.** Despite their intangible contributions as employees, servant leaders consider people to be valuable on an internal level. As a result, the servant leader is utterly dedicated to the personal development of each and every member of his or her organization.

In *Character and Servant Leadership: Ten Characteristics of Effective Caring Leaders,* Larry Spears, a former president of the Robert K. Greenleaf Center for Servant Leadership, outlines the traits that a servant leader must possess to be effective. Empathy, listening, healing, awareness, persuasion, conceptualization, foresight, stewardship, commitment to people's growth, and community building are some of these qualities.

In an article for the *University of Nebraska Faculty Publications,* two researchers, John E. Barbuto and Daniel W. Wheeler, combined Spears'

10 traits into a framework known as "the natural desire to serve others." This framework divides Spears' 10 traits into five dimensions of servant leadership, including altruistic calling, emotional healing, wisdom, persuasive mapping, and organizational stewardship.

In his book *Servant Leadership in the Workplace,* Joe Iarocci outlines what servant leadership entails in the workplace, outlining three key priorities (developing people, creating a trusted team, and achieving results), three key principles (serve first, persuasion, empowerment), and three key practices (listening, delegating, and connecting followers to mission).

The nine "functional attributes of servant leadership" that Robert F. Russell and Gregory A. Stone, two researchers, developed and published in the *Leadership & Organization Development Journal* include vision, honesty, integrity, trust, service, modelling, pioneering, appreciation of others, and empowerment. They also listed 11 "accompanying traits," which include delegation, communication, credibility, competence, stewardship, visibility, influence, and persuasion.

The Traits of Servant Leadership

According to Greenleaf, servant leaders are less concerned in concentrating on profits and simply telling people what to do and more interested in meeting the needs of employees and assisting them in developing within the firm. In their book *Seven Pillars of Servant Leadership: Practicing the Wisdom of Leading by Serving,* researchers James Sipe and Don Frick, who studied Greenleaf's work, identified seven servant leadership pillars that fall within the purview of his original theory but are not specifically outlined by him. These pillars include:

- **Personal character**: A servant leader upholds integrity, bases decisions on morals and values, exemplifies humility, and works toward a higher goal inside the organization.

- **Puts people first:** A servant leader shows concern and care for others while assisting staff members in achieving their objectives and progressing within the company.

- **Effective communicator:** Effective communication with your staff is essential to servant leadership, so be sure you can communicate with them, listen to them, and invite input.

- **Compassionate collaborator:** In order to be a successful servant leader, you must regularly collaborate with people to build connections, encourage diversity, equity, and inclusion, and manage conflict in the workplace.

- **Is visionary:** As a servant leader, you must look to the future and foresee any potential effects on the organization. Additionally, you'll need to have a clear vision for your business and possess the ability to move decisively when necessary.

- **Systems thinker:** Servant leaders need to be able to adapt to change and feel at ease navigating complicated surroundings. Strategic thinking and the capacity to effectively drive organizational change are prerequisites for this kind of leadership.

- **Leads with moral authority:** As a servant leader, it's critical to build trust and confidence among your team members by establishing high standards, taking on and assigning responsibility, and promoting an accountability-friendly culture.

The qualities of servant leadership include the capacity to let go of perceived wrongdoings and not carry a grudge into subsequent situations, as well as the capacity to comprehend and experience the sentiments of others and where they are coming from. Setting up a trusting environment where people feel accepted, can make errors without fear of repercussions is crucial for servant leaders.

In his article on servant leadership that was published in the *Journal of Management,* Dirk van Dierendonck argued that leaders who demonstrate humility by admitting they do not have all the answers, being true to themselves, and adopting an accepting interpersonal attitude create a work environment where followers feel safe and trusted. According to Van Dierendonck, servant leaders use influence and persuasion in their conversations with followers to develop this high-quality relationship, rather than directives and orders.

The theories of transformational leadership and authentic leadership are sometimes contrasted with those of servant leadership.

It's interesting how the transformational method highlights the leader's ethical responsibilities and draws attention to the necessity of leaders communicating vision in a morally and ethically sound manner. The capacity to convey a fair understanding of other viewpoints or sides of an issue while acting in accordance with one's genuine self is mentioned as being a quality of the authentic leader.

Previous studies indicate that servant leadership supports employees' emotional healing, which fosters their emotional wellbeing. Additionally, it has been asserted in the past that emotional intelligence (EI) and well-being are linked. According to the studies, those with high EI are happier, more confident, more optimistic, and more satisfied. According to recent studies, servant leadership improves employees' emotional intelligence (EI) and overall welfare.

Final Thoughts and Questions to Consider

Servant leadership is a radical departure from the predominant style and history of leadership in our organizations, which has been much more focused on a "command-and-control" approach.

Questions to Consider

1. What changes would be needed in moving toward a servant leadership model in the organization you are in?

2. How would you determine if a potential leader believes in and can practice servant leadership? Either in the recruitment and hiring process or promotion?

Chapter 8

The Humble Leader

"Be gentle and you can be bold; be frugal and you can be liberal; avoid putting yourself before others and you can become a leader among men."

— Laozi

The research on moral and ethical leaders point to those who are honest and humble. The more honesty and humility employees may have, the higher their job performance, as rated by the employees' supervisor. That's the new finding from a Baylor University study published in the journal *Personality and Individual Differences* that found the honesty-humility personality traits was a unique predictor of job performance.

"Researchers already know that integrity can predict job performance and what we are saying here is that humility and honesty are also major components in that," said Dr. Wade Rowatt, associate professor of psychology and neuroscience at Baylor, who helped lead the study. "This study shows that those who possess the combination of honesty and humility have better job performance. In fact, we found that humility and honesty not only correspond with job performance, but it predicted job performance above and beyond any of the other five personality traits like agreeableness and conscientiousness."

Humble leaders are more effective and better liked, according to a study published in the *Academy of Management Journal*. "Leaders of all ranks view admitting mistakes, spotlighting follower strengths and modelling teachability as being at the core of humble leadership" says Bradley Owens, assistant professor of organization and human resources at the University at Buffalo School of Management. A follow-up study published in the journal *Organization Science*, using data from more than 700 employees and 218 leaders, confirmed that leader humility is associated with more learning-oriented teams, more engaged employees and lower voluntary employee turnover.

In an article in the *Harvard Business Review* entitled "Level 5 Leadership: The Triumph of Humility and Fierce Resolve," leadership expert Jim Collins argues the best leaders exhibit humility, shunning public adulation and are never boastful. In a widely read *Harvard Business Review* publication, Collins explained that the personal humility of Level 5 Leaders was typified by: A compelling modesty about their accomplishments; quiet determination rather than charisma; ambition focused on the company rather than self; willingness to accept personal responsibility for failures; and acknowledgment of the role of others in achieving success.

There's a clear connection between moral and ethical behavior in leaders and their humility, according to F.O Walumbwa, and J. Schaubroeck writing in the *Journal of Applied Psychology*. They conclude, "Leaders who are humble in their character and model humility in their actions, create the opposite kind of environment to that of the amoral unethical leader. This environment is grounded in respect, tolerance, and outcomes that are mutually beneficial for the firm and for the individual. Leaders who are good role models tend to radiate positivity, and instead of spawning a downward spiral, they create an upward spiral that elevates pro-social employee behaviors."

Jennifer Cole Wright in her edited book, *Humility*, says, "The central problem with low humility is not that people think that they are better than others. People low in humility expect others to treat them as special; try to reap social benefits that they don't deserve; and their sense of entitlement leads them to behave in self-centered ways that disadvantage other people."

In contrast, humble people who do not put themselves above others, or expect preferential treatment, or think they are entitled to a disproportionate share of any benefits, and are more likely to treat others in an egalitarian, respectful, and fair manner, Wright argues.

All theorists agree that humility is associated with an array of prosocial behaviors, and studies support this connection. For example, humility is associated with gratitude, willingness to help others, empathy, forgiveness and success in working and communicating with others. In close relationships, humble people display greater skill at conflict resolution and are more likely to make sacrifices for others and they display more trust, greater cooperation, and less conflict.

Researchers Yanhan Zhu and colleagues studied the relationship between humble leadership and employee resilience and productivity which was published in *Frontiers of Psychology*. They concluded: "Humble leaderships can be defined as: a leadership style in which a leader evaluates him/herself and subordinates through a multifaceted and objective lens, appreciating subordinates' positive worth, strengths, and contributions. It contains three behavioral components: (a) a willingness to acknowledge one's limits and mistakes; (b) shining a spotlight on employees' contributions and strengths; and (c) keeping openness to advice, ideas, and feedback."

Edgar H. Schein and Peter A. Schein in their research and published study, *Humble Leadership: The Power of Relationships, Openness and Trust,* argue that the growing complexity of the modern world requires stronger workplace relationships in order to accomplish tasks. The authors argue that the changing world necessitates humble leadership due to the changing nature of work:

- Leadership will become more about *context* and *process* rather than *content* and *expertise.*

- Humble Leadership can help overcome unconscious biases, segregation, and exclusion.

- Individual abuse of power is tempting. Humble leaders have a better track record of resisting the abuse of power in comparison with leaders with low humility.

- Humble leadership can help facilitate the movement toward agile organizations.

The authors make the salient point that the workplace now puts a premium on so-called "soft-skills" and experimental learning, and is moving away from authoritarian and one-size fits all training and development. They say that it's the leader's responsibility to foster those dynamics correctly by introducing the right tasks at the right time and at the right pace. A humble leader's effectiveness will depend on how well you can incorporate soft skills into the group dynamic so your group can accomplish even its most complex goals.

According to research published in *Organization Science* by Michael Johnson and colleagues from the University of Washington Foster School of Business, using data from more than 700 employees and 218 leaders, confirmed that leader humility is associated with more learning-oriented teams, more engaged employees and lower voluntary employee turnover.

Humble leaders are more effective and better liked, according to a study published in the *Academy of Management Journal.* "Leaders of all ranks view admitting mistakes, spotlighting follower strengths and modelling "teachability" as being at the core of humble leadership" says Bradley Owens, assistant professor of organization and human resources at the University at Buffalo School of Management.

The more honesty and humility an employee may have, the higher their job performance, as rated by the employees' supervisor, according to a Baylor University study published in the journal *Personality and Individual Differences* by Wade Rowatt, associate professor of psychology and neuroscience. He found humility was a unique predictor of job performance.

Amy Y. Ou and her colleagues at Arizona State University published a study in *Administrative Science Quarterly*, examined the leadership traits associated with Confucianism, with a focus on humility. Those traits include self-awareness, openness to feedback, and a focus on the greater good and others' welfare, as opposed to dwelling on oneself. Ou and her colleagues argue the self-awareness of humble leaders enables them to be open-minded and willing to learn, to appreciate both their own strengths and weaknesses as well as those of others, and to transcend the self in the pursuit of a higher and more significant objective while continuing to improve.

Ou and colleagues concluded "Accordingly, humility provides integration of both high self-knowledge and low self-focus in terms of identifying personal priorities about goal achievement." They contend humble leaders' "life pursuits are less about themselves than about the larger community, the greater whole, moral principles, or ultimate universal truth."

Joseph Folkman writes in a report, "How Do You Become an Effective Leader? Stay Humble," a follow up to a previous article on humble leaders in *Harvard Business Review,* argues "How do people make the judgment that a leader is arrogant or humble? Arrogant leaders don't parade around with a badge indicating they are conceited. Yet, there is a high degree of consensus within organizations about who is humble and who is arrogant. The reality is that there are a set of very predictable behaviors that send clear signals about an individual's humility or arrogance."

Folkman studied 1,072 leaders and concluded the following:

- **On a general leadership performance index, humble leaders are ranked higher than arrogant leaders.** A comparison of the 54 behaviors that set apart the most effective leaders from the least effective leaders on a general leadership effectiveness index. The 34th percentile was assigned to haughty leaders, while the 66th percentile was given to arrogant ones.

- **Humble leaders showed that the importance of people is equal to that of outcomes.** The arrogant leader thinks that getting results is the main objective and that any unfavorable effects on a few people are just a necessary evil. The modest leaders know how to strike a balance between success and sensitivity to the needs of each individual. They also think that by taking care of individuals, you may increase their commitment and engagement, which will eventually lead to greater outcomes.

- **Humble leaders who put others' trust as their top priority.** Humble leaders go above and beyond to foster mutual trust. They are more successful at establishing trust by forging strong bonds with others, continuously keeping their word, and demonstrating knowledge and sound judgement.

- **Humble leaders think that cooperation and teamwork are the keys to success.** The conceited leader thinks they can achieve their objectives on their own. They don't want to work together because they want to take the credit. The modest leaders understand that cooperation among employees is the key to corporate success. They refuse to take credit for other people's successes and instead ask others for assistance.

- **Humble leaders serve as examples and practice what they preach.** Humble leaders make sure they do the task before asking others to do it. Leaders with arrogance are okay with requesting that others perform duties that they themselves do not perform. They don't perceive the double standard, or they are okay with it. Arrogant leaders frequently behave as though they belong to a special class to whom the laws that apply to everyone else do not.

- **Humble leaders get feedback from others and act on it.** Humble leaders solicit feedback from others and make a sincere effort to put their recommendations for improvement into action. Leaders with arrogance believe they don't need or desire feedback from others. In fact, they frequently believe that requesting feedback would imply that they lack confidence in themselves. They therefore refuse to inquire.

- **Humble leaders find constructive solutions to disputes.** Conflict with others is frequently a result of haughty leaders. This is caused, in part, by the idea that conflict encourages others to become more competitive. Humble leaders strive to overcome disagreements because they believe that confrontation fosters a toxic work atmosphere.

- **Humble leaders offer constructive criticism to others.** The haughty leaders think it is their responsibility to judge others and point out their errors. Almost always, they provide unfavorable and corrective criticism. The modest leader is aware that performance evaluations must be based on truthful feedback.

Scholars and professionals alike have suggested that today's leaders must approach their positions with more humility. Recent leadership theories have started to concentrate more emphasis on the bottom-up components of leadership as a result of workplace complexity and quick changes that demand adaptability from leaders. Some experts even contend that the fundamental concept of leadership needs to be altered, including what it is, how it functions, and even how people may recognize it when they see it.

Researchers have also recommended that leaders move past the "great man" or "hero myth" theories of leadership by focusing more on how followers affect the leadership process and exhibiting their humanity by being honest about their knowledge and experience gaps.

Recently, several academics and experts have urged professionals and leaders across all professions to take a more humble attitude to their jobs. For instance, judges and attorneys must be humble in order to interpret the law correctly and strike a balance between the concepts of mercy and justice.

Competence and humility are regarded as the two primary characteristics of medical professionalism. For political and military leaders, humility has also been highlighted as being crucial, particularly in the current political context.

Humble leadership can be included into bottom-up, participatory leadership. Although some favor top-down approaches to strategic transformation, others are now advocating that businesses must learn to "grow strategy from below" and pursue "little victories" from the bottom up, as shown by the agile leadership paradigm.

The servant leader and humble leadership theories have many things in common. Servant leaders see the growth of their followers as a goal in and of itself, rather than as a way to further their own or the organization's objectives.

Leaders who humbly acknowledge they do not need to be the master of all skills and communicating to others they have much to contribute in achieving an optimal result also builds organizational commitment and increases trust in the leader argue researchers Robert S. Dennis and Mihal Bocarnea. Not only does accurate self-knowledge recognize one's own values, they argue, but humble leaders fully recognize the importance of others' values and priorities — including the big picture capacity to pursue a better future that can come from collaborative action, and the necessity of creating strong partnerships with others to achieve that optimal future.

Final Thoughts and Questions to Consider

Extensive research has shown that humble leaders in general achieve better and longer lasting positive results in their organizations, and get the respect and cooperation from their employees.

Here Are Some Questions to Consider

1. Why do you think that employers and Boards are not hiring or promoting humble, less extroverted leaders? How can this change?

2. How can research about humble leaders success become more mainstream?

Chapter 9

Spiritual Leadership Theory and Character Development

"Spiritual growth requires the development of inner knowing and inner authority. It requires the heart, not the intellect."

— Gary Zukav

A developing paradigm that connects leadership and spirituality is known as spiritual leadership theory. **In this sense, the term "spiritual" refers to acknowledging and nurturing the essence or animating energy that underpins human nature.** The majority of the thought presented in this area is drawn from the disciplines of leadership ethics and values and religious theology and practice. Motivating and inspiring followers to love and serve others is a key component of spiritual leadership. To date, a wide range of institutions, including secondary schools, a university, military units, local governments, police, and for-profit enterprises, have tested the notion of spiritual leadership. According to the findings of these studies, the spiritual leadership model has a beneficial impact on employee life happiness, organizational dedication and productivity, various work unit performance metrics, and sales growth.

Internal Development and Character

Inner-life practices help people develop their essential values as well as the character development elements of self-identity, self-awareness, feeling of agency, and self-control. An inner life practice that gives people insights into who they are, where they find meaning in life (purpose), how they want to live a life that matters, and the importance of the contributions they are making is the root of spiritual leadership. People can improve their inner life by doing things like spending time in nature, praying, meditating, reading inspirational books, doing yoga, adhering to religious traditions, looking up role models, keeping a journal, working out, and reflecting on their experiences.

Identities and Core Beliefs.

Establishing the essential beliefs and self-identity required for character is rooted in love and service to others requires inner-life practices, such as self-reflection. People get insights into their identities through inner reflection, outside criticism, and observation of role models. Core values and beliefs become integrated with self-identity when people utilize them to define who they are and set developmental goals. Their thoughts, motivation, and conduct are then positively impacted by a greater knowledge of their basic beliefs and self-identity.

Feeling of Agency.

A person's feeling of agency or commitment to fortify his or her character and to live and lead in accordance with sound fundamental principles that advance the common good is also increased through inner-life practices. Assuming control of their character-building journeys and having the confidence to be open and honest with themselves are prerequisites for this. People who have agency actively participate in activities that strengthen their character. The transition from independent, self-focused identities to interdependent, other-focused identities is aided by agency. A person becomes more susceptible to finding significance or a calling in working toward loftier objectives that benefit the greater good as a result of this shift in how they define themselves in relation to serving others. Additionally, the agency that is built via inner-life activities helps people make moral decisions and act in ways that are consistent with their underlying beliefs and sense of self.

Self-Awareness.

Inner-life techniques help people become more self-aware by strengthening their capacity to observe and regulate their thoughts, feelings, and behavior. People can transition from having excellent intentions to acting honorably with the help of their capacity to observe and comprehend their thoughts and the origins of their sentiments. For instance, mindfulness, which one develops via inner-life activities, is the capacity to pay attention to and be open to what is occurring in one's immediate experience with care and discernment. Through mindfulness, one learns to recognize self-imposed, false assumptions and limitations that impede growth as well as to acquire insight into the real path that ultimately leads to expansion of potential and contentment. An individual's moral and ethical decisions and acts are guided by their understanding of their own values and beliefs.

Self-Regulation.

Inner-life practices also help people become more adept at understanding and managing their emotions, thoughts, and—most importantly—behavior. One learns about their cognitive patterns, emotional triggers, and motivations for their actions through introspection and mindfulness. The ability to constantly match one's thoughts and behaviors with one's underlying beliefs and self-identity and so display character is made possible by these insights.

Spiritual Direction

The character development components of social awareness, self-motivation, fundamental values, and self-identity are all facilitated by spiritual leadership. The combination of a leader's vision, genuine concern for the welfare of the group (altruistic love), and hope and faith produces spiritual leadership. Leaders who create compelling visions based on upholding organizational principles while serving a higher purpose give their followers guidance, motivation to accomplish a noble goal, and, most importantly, a sense of purpose in their work.

This assists leaders in fostering trust and boosting worker motivation by showing genuine concern for the well-being and growth of group members. Last but not least, executives who are upbeat give their team members optimism and faith in a better future for both the company and themselves. The optimism and faith that people have in a better future gives those with whom they work the drive to excel and change for the better, and it also strengthens their loyalty to the company.

A deep motivational force within employees to improve themselves and the organization is sparked by a leader who fosters an organizational climate that is characterized by caring, a vision that inspires people to serve a higher purpose, and group members' hope and faith regarding their professional and personal development. These higher-order influences on spiritual leadership behaviors are quite comparable to transformational leadership behaviors such as individual consideration and inspiring motivation.

Vision and Social Consciousness.

Vision is crucial for the development of leaders. Leaders are given a purpose that goes beyond self-interest and direction in their pursuits of personal development when they have a vision of leading and living in accordance with their values and beliefs while also serving others. Leaders must cultivate social awareness and the interpersonal skills essential to build a vision of honesty and service to others. Leaders are aware that their capability to interact favorably with others enhances their ability to exert influence and help others. Leaders are able to reach their potential through social awareness and relationships with others.

Optimism and Faith

Additionally, a leader who instils higher levels of optimism and faith can help group members envision stronger versions of themselves in the future, which tends to boost their drive to strive toward achieving the end goal of being individuals of good character. As a result, the main sources of internal motivation in the development of character are hope and faith. They provide people the willpower to keep pursuing the objective of strengthening and acting in accordance with their character despite social temptations to do otherwise. Hope is linked to improved performance at work in addition to being crucial for character development.

Altruistic Love, Fundamental Principles, and Sense of Self.

Altruistic love is characterized for spiritual leadership as profound concern, love, and admiration for oneself and others that results in a sense of wholeness, harmony, and wellbeing. Honesty, integrity, humility, courage, and compassion are qualities that often encourage altruistic love. Leaders who embody these principles are more likely to lead in a way that shows their genuine care and concern for their followers, creating an environment that encourages trust.

Altruistic love, which underpins care, concern, and appreciation in the workplace, encourages candor and encourages employees to take calculated risks in order to reach their full potential. This profound level of concern is comparable to unconditional positive regard, as defined by Carl Rogers in 1961. When leaders value their employees for who they are and encourage them to develop their full potential, people tend to flourish.

Putting Spiritual Leadership into Action.

In order to nurture character development through hope/faith in a vision to serve others through altruistic love, consultants and leaders might employ a variety of strategies. Jim Collins and Jerry Porras' description of the vision generation process is highly effective for articulating an organization's basic values and purpose, fostering consensus, and constructing an enthralling future state. This method encourages group members to consider their own values, beliefs, and identities as well as those of the organization. Members are prompted to reflect on their reasons for holding certain values and views, as well as their identities and the ways in which these values and beliefs are expressed in the workplace. People must consider their life's purpose and significance as well as their ability to make a difference in order to imagine a future end-state that is deserving of their efforts. A climate that meets people's spiritual needs is more likely to be created by organizations that use this process to clarify their core values, align employees' understanding of them, and win members' commitment. Participation at all levels is essential to the success of the vision formulation process.

It makes sense for leaders to encourage people to adopt Collins and Porras' process to design their personal development plans, which will then incorporate their life visions. An individual's vision, like an organization's, can give group members the path to take so they can achieve their potential selves, the reason for moving in that direction, and the drive to keep growing.

The search for meaning through moving beyond self-interests to associate with and serve something bigger that advances the common good is at the core of the vision. This connection to something greater can include being a member of an organization that serves others or the general good. Alternatively, the association with something bigger than oneself may involve a supreme, sacred, and divine power or deity, depending on one's religious views. This relationship with a higher power or deity can give people meaning and purpose, prosocial principles, guidelines for living, and a source of strength and consolation while facing challenges.

Leaders who are upbeat about the future of the company and the people they lead can increase the hope and faith of their followers. They must provide a positive example, grow the group and the organization to meet emerging difficulties, guarantee that all operations are conducted morally and ethically, and articulate a compelling future (vision) for all group members and the organization. The optimism and faith of a group's members that they will become better team members and individuals in the future is increased by leaders who believe in the potential of their team members, serve as positive role models, and invest in developing this potential.

Additionally, leaders can encourage optimism in employees' personal development plans by requiring them to define unique goals. Leaders examine these developmental plans with employees during recurring developmental counselling meetings to assess progress, decide whether and how to offer more support, create backup plans, and change goals as necessary. These admirable actions show leaders' belief in a better future, which may strengthen group members' faith, hope, motivation, and resiliency in pursuing their own goals.

Through fidelity and unselfish service, leaders show their genuine love and concern for others. They take care of their workers' best interests, offer them support when they make errors, and spend time coaching and mentoring them to help them grow as individuals. Regular developmental counselling sessions led by compassionate leaders result in insightful discussions and resource-friendly development plans. Additionally, they make themselves available to their staff by roaming around and maintaining open door policy.

Caring leaders solicit the opinions of the group's participants, encourage their initiative, share information with them to foster transparency, and involve them in the process of formulating the strategic direction. Offering flexibility in the work schedule to accommodate family needs, providing different career tracks for employees with different family obligations, establishing a coaching program, creating a wellness team to provide input on how to improve the work environment, hosting periodic retreats and social events to foster team spirit are all additional ways to show care for others.

Good Spiritual Health

Spiritual leadership supports the group's members' spiritual well-being in regard to membership and meaning/calling. People can discover meaning in their job and even in their lives when leaders present a compelling vision based on principles and service to a higher purpose. Individuals must put aside their self-interests in order to work together for a goal bigger than themselves in order to serve a better purpose. Group members shift from being egocentric to becoming other-centric in order to achieve a higher goal of advancing the welfare of all members.

People might experience a feeling of purpose and calling in their lives when they transcend their own interests and work toward the greater good. Similar to this, people come together in a noble pursuit when they work toward a greater cause or superior objective. This can increase people's desire to be a part of the business when coupled with a culture that is founded on values, care, and acceptance. Members of the group experience a sense of belonging and acceptance from others, which satisfies their fundamental need for attachment.

In terms of character development, being part of a team that upholds ideals and working toward a greater good can help people find fulfilment in their careers and personal lives. A person's identity may be impacted to the point that they begin to regard themselves as someone who works for the good of others by engaging in behaviors that advance a greater good. Similar to this, persons who have a strong desire to fit in with a group are more inclined to adhere to its standards and beliefs. Thus, an organization seeking a higher purpose can have a positive impact on members' values and beliefs, identities, and worldviews through the social identity hypothesis.

Leaders must constantly connect the daily actions of their staff to the greater goal after developing a compelling vision for their organizations. Members of the group are able to perceive how their everyday actions contribute to the organization and its goals thanks to the leaders' consistent framing and meaning-making.

Advancement Toward the Larger Goal.

Another strategy leaders can utilize to foster a sense of belonging and significance among their workforce is to support local, national, and international volunteerism. Most people aspire to work for or join a group that benefits society because it gives them purpose in both their professional and personal life. Leaders can use participatory decision making, team-building exercises like sports and games to promote cohesion, peer coaching, recognizing employees' contributions to the workplace and the community, hosting family events, and holding periodic group meals with the sole intention of fostering relationships to further improve membership.

Personal Results

In addition to membership and purpose, the individual or personal results connected to spiritual leadership also include better productivity, a greater sense of psychological well-being, and higher levels of life satisfaction. Research findings unmistakably show that spiritual leadership benefits both organizations and their constituents.

Putting Inner-Life Techniques into Action.

Consultants and leaders can employ a range of strategies to encourage inner-life activities in the workplace and promote character development. These include encouraging employees to keep a developmental journal, facilitating employees to identify their core values and beliefs and compare these with the company's core values during developmental counselling, and providing employees with assessment measures such as personality, leadership style, character strengths, and leadership ability. Other organizational-level strategies that leaders can use include designating a space in the office for inner silence, giving staff members a safe space to talk about challenging spiritual topics, encouraging and supporting meditative practices, having spiritual advisors on call, facilitating the formation of support groups, and establishing a reading room where group members can access spiritual literature .

Chapter 10

A Tale of Two Leaders

"True leadership is moral authority, not formal authority. Leadership is a choice, not a position. The choice is to follow universal timeless principles, which will build trust and respect from the entire organization. Those with formal authority alone will lose this trust and respect."

— Stephen R. Covey

In my book, *I Know Myself and Neither Do You,* I profile two senior executives who I coached, showing the contrast between a good leader and a bad one. While the focus was on their differing levels of self-awareness, there were also some glaring differences with respect to ethical behavior that relates to the need for good character.

Robert (the "bad" leader)

The first leader (I'll refer to him as "Robert")was the young executive of a large international company, who had been with the company for 5 years. When I was first engaged to be his coach, his boss, the CEO and I had a good extensive discussion during which the CEO expressed concern about reports he had been getting from employees about leadership style, and behaviors. He suggested I meet with Robert and see if the two of us would be agreeable to working together. I said that I would, and I set up a meeting with Robert a week later.

When I first met Robert in his office, I was struck by some immediate impressions. First, he was a physically imposing man in his mid-30s--tall, handsome, with a palatable energy of confidence and command. He had a business degree and MBA, but had not distinguished himself as a student. While involved in his MBA program, he had also been working as an entrepreneur, creating a start-up which had created a business tool app for busy executives. The company was successful, and within three years was bought out by a large corporation. In many ways Robert was a stereotypical leader of a Silicon Valley company--brash, aggressive, bold and creative.

As I came to learn in the ensuing months, he was clearly driven, impatient, intolerant of others and insensitive to their feelings. His rapid-fire manner of speaking, almost in bullet points, was a reflection of his style.

As I was to find out, Robert had a small loyal core of supporters, most of whom supported and tolerated him for personal gain, and then there was a much larger group of employees, colleagues and others who disliked and distrusted Robert.

When Robert first arrived at the company, he quickly made drastic strategic, organization and personnel changes in the areas of his responsibility.

These changes had produced some small immediate successes, and on the other hand, had alienated a significant number of employees; not involved them in any way in the planning of changes; and some of whom showed their displeasure by leaving the company. In addition, his plans were poorly designed and rarely reached completion. When the lack of success was obvious, Robert blamed others for the shortcomings.

When confronted with the negative feedback, Robert's response was that the only measure that he or the Board cared about was the bottom-line performance for shareholders, and in that, he was successful.

Quickly his intemperate reputation spread, and the kind of people he attracted both in his personal and business lives tended to be those whose prime motive was either self-interest, or an "ends-justifies-the-means" philosophy. Robert was idolized by his fans for his personality, but not competence and sometimes feared by his competitors for his ruthlessness.

In our initial coaching sessions, Robert quickly tried to establish dominance and take control of the sessions, as he did with most relationships. I had been around enough other executives with similar behavior patterns to recognize that I had to challenge him immediately. I confronted him about his attempts, indicating that if our relationship was not to be one of equals, I would withdraw from the coaching arrangement and that I would tell his boss that he was non-cooperative. That response seemed to gain credibility with him, and he modified his behavior accordingly, although, like all bad habits, he couldn't resist lapsing back into this default behavior occasionally.

It was clear to me that one of the major problems Robert had was his lack of self-awareness, and that was having a significant negative impact on others. In addition, I shared with him feedback I had received from his subordinates about the aggressive and dismissive attitude they had received from him during discussions.

In the first few coaching sessions we had, he started to become more open to the importance of raising his self-awareness, emotional intelligence and more open to the value of feedback from others. In a rare moment of vulnerability and honesty with himself and me, he admitted that sometimes he felt he was a fraud, and he was deathly afraid of being "found out" for being a fraud and phony. I asked him if he was okay about that observation and did he want to do anything about it. I felt here was an opening where he could commit to change. Then in an instant, the look of vulnerability on his face was gone, and he returned to his usual overconfident arrogant persona.

Robert's unethical behavior was illustrated by two ongoing events. The first was his interaction with potential investors, where he was "caught" making false and misleading statements about investment opportunities and subsequent communications. The second was his commitment to the CEO to provide timely information about the financial division's organizational policies and procedures. Robert repeatedly promised to complete these on time and effectively, and rather than taking responsibility for not doing so, continued to obfuscate, lie about his efforts, and not fulfill his commitments.

After I worked with Robert for almost a year, the CEO finally terminated Robert's employment, having given up on a belief in any improvement, despite Robert's work with me.

Using the criteria for leadership demonstrating virtuous behavior and good character Robert exhibited the following:

Character/Virtue	Behavior Exhibited
Knowledge/Wisdom	Exhibited no interest in learning new things
Honesty/Integrity/Trustworthiness	Lied and deceived; was not trusted by employees, CEO and potential investors
Justice/Fairness	Played favorites with his employees
Temperance	Was impulsive, rash, with emotional outbursts
Humility	Hubris, arrogance
Collaboration	Tried to do everything himself
Accountability/Responsibility	Blamed others for problems and mistakes
Courage	Lacked the courage to initiate changes to fix things
Judgment	Poor judgment in work tasks, and people

Daniel

Daniel is a C-Suite Executive in his mid-50s in a large international manufacturing company. He had varied experiences in different industries including the financial services sector in an HR capacity, but had been promoted into operations with wide-ranging responsibilities including the key advisor to the CEO.

His personal life was as important as his work life, as was evident from him limiting his work hours and putting his family first over work. In addition, Daniel had a wide circle of friends that he had known for many years, and he was also actively involved in the community.

Daniel had engaged me as his coach while he was at his previous company, and when he joined the manufacturing company, he asked me to continue to work with him and I agreed.

While Daniel's technical and organizational skills are outstanding, he was known for the strength of his interpersonal relationships with employees, peers and colleagues and business associates.

While Daniel's warm and open personality was a big contributor to his success, he has intentionally engaged in behaviors that have augmented his emotional intelligence, including engaging a coach, regularly taking time to reflect on his inner state and emotions, and taking action on 360 assessments where there was a gap between others' and his own perceptions.

As a result, the trust level personal commitment that Daniel enjoyed with others was very high.

He was always thinking and acting about how to empower, enable and support his people. A secondary result is that Daniel's reputation travelled far beyond his company, so that he became a very desirable talent in the executive workplace, and was approached several times by recruitment head-hunters for other positions.

During our coaching sessions, Daniel was open to any tool or practice that would increase his self-awareness, and engaged in a program of regular reflection time, solitude retreats and "doing nothing" to enhance his creativity.

Daniel had already engaged in considerable work to raise his self-awareness, both with me and on his own. Our sessions, assessments and personal goals continued to enhance his willingness to see his blind spots, be vulnerable, and relate to his employees and colleagues with compassion, kindness and empathy.

Using the criteria for leadership demonstrating virtuous behavior and good character Daniel exhibited the following:

Character/Virtue	Behavior Exhibited
Knowledge/Wisdom	Engaged in an ongoing learning and development program; prodigious reader.
Honesty/Integrity/Trustworthiness	High level of integrity, honesty; was trusted by all and good for his word.

Justice/Fairness	Treated his employees, vendors and colleagues fairly and equitably.
Temperance	Exhibited strong emotional regulation, and was never reactive or impulsive.
Humility	A humble person, letting others take credit; a servant leader.
Collaboration	Sought others' input and open-minded
Accountability/Responsibility	Took responsibility for mistakes and gave credit to others for successes.
Courage	Confronted both employees and others when dealing with ethical issues and difficult decisions.
Judgment	Exercised good judgment in decisions. Also, not quick to judge or criticize others.

Chapter 11

Character and Virtues Based Leadership Development

"Leadership always begins with the inner person. People sense the depth of a person's character."

— John C. Maxwell

The majority of organizations do not design their leadership development and training programs with "building character" or developing virtues in mind. John Adair claims in his *Action Centered Leadership Model* that developing leaders transcends organizational boundaries because it happens in families, schools, and universities; nonetheless, but it is up to organizations to do this. Adair advises hiring managers to look for individuals who exhibit traits of character including honesty, dependability, and stability as well as leadership and teamwork skills, decision-making skills, communication skills, and self-management skills. Adair goes on to say that these candidates need to be educated and prepared to collaborate effectively in order to perform the role of a leader.

While there is a dearth of literature on the multifaceted construction of character development, research on the growth of many aspects of character, particularly in the workplace, have been conducted. Pamela Sue Hartman discovered that the formation of wisdom is preceded by the accumulation of a wide variety of adult experiences, just as she discovered in her study published in her book, *Women Developing*

Wisdom. These might include successful crisis and adversity resolution, as well as mentorship in the workplace. Another illustration is perseverance, which grows as a result of social support, getting praise and rewards, and exercising self-control. For instance, it is well known that social support offered by diversity and multiculturalism variety promotes the development of personal integrity.

According to a study on perceived leader integrity and subordinates' ethical intentions, subordinates who do not subscribe to a belief in universal moral values had lower inclinations to engage in unethical behavior as their leaders' perceived integrity rose. This suggests that a leader's character directly affects whether or not followers will engage in unethical behavior, thereby fostering character in the workplace. By encouraging mutual disclosure of goals and values, encouraging a leader of character to do the same, and agreeing to reciprocal feedback and mutual accountability in their performance improvement activities, a leader of character can further impact their followers.

How to Include Character and Virtues in Programs for Leadership Development

The social networks one is a part of are where one develops their character. Organizational cultures, from families to businesses, have an impact on a person's moral principles, self-identity, and attitudes toward morality. They can also help or hinder the development of a person's character strengths, offer social support for moral or immoral behavior, and hold a person accountable for moral and ethical behavior. Therefore, a person should choose groups whose values and views are compatible with their own in order to boost the development of their character.

Organizations with moral and ethical cultures express their values in a way that makes it apparent what they stand for and the kind of future they want to build as well as their vision and purpose. Before joining, members of these organizations must pledge to act morally and ethically, and they have standards and processes in place to make sure everyone follows them. Members of these groups help and motivate one another to lead moral lives. In order to ensure moral and ethical behavior among its members, an organization's shared values are reflected in its culture and rules. These values act as both a support system and a kind of social control.

Organizations should implement methods to identify and reward moral behavior, discipline immoral behavior, and promote a moral and ethical culture.

Additionally, moral groups have leaders who work as role models to spread their views and ideals as well as coaches and mentors to help members of the group grow as people. Leaders provide meaning about why moral and ethical behavior is vital to the organization and to each group member's identity through coaching and mentoring sessions as well as daily contacts. One of the most effective ways leaders may help followers develop their character is by offering group members situations (real or case studies) that test their values and beliefs, giving them feedback and support, and then coaching them through the experience's reflection.

The Values Project (TVP) suggested one strategy for emphasizing character and virtues in leadership development. It focuses on pedagogically oriented learning and teaching methods that create character by fostering virtues. The following are the five tactics in the TVP that could be utilized to create both present and future leaders:

TVP Strategy 1: Use the Virtues' Language

This indicates that when speaking with the current or aspiring leader, the trainer or mentor employs the language of values. This entails recognizing and acknowledging the virtues that are latent in a person's behavior, as well as seeing and hearing such virtues. This increases the ability of that individual to recognize that they possess that virtue and that they have the option of choosing to employ it in their future actions. Speaking the Language of Virtues is predicated on the idea that what we say and how we speak to one another shapes who and how we become, and that recognizing virtues strengthens moral character and self-assurance. While pleasant and relational in tone, speaking the Language of Virtues does not imply avoiding challenging or critical talks. Instead of using harsh language or completely avoiding a dialogue, this tactic is intended to guide and correct conduct through introducing a person to values.

In TVP's Educator Guide from 2005, the value of "catching somebody in the act of doing a virtue" is emphasized. This entails looking for situations where people are putting a virtue into practice that does not come naturally to them. A person who is typically shy may be "caught" for his boldness when he speaks up in a meeting, or a person who is typically task-focused may be commended for her compassion when she expresses concern for a colleague.

Speaking the Language of Virtues consists of three sections and can be used to (1) acknowledgment of behavior, (2) description of the behavior, and (3) commend the appropriate behaviors or suggest how the inappropriate behavior be corrected.

For instance, a leader can make a virtues appreciation by saying, "(1) thank you for (2) the determination (3) you demonstrated in your sustained efforts to get make progress on the project," if an employee has demonstrated diligence and productivity. However, if an employee missed the first project deadline, the manager could give moral advice by saying, "(1) you need to be (2) responsible (3) in achieving your deadlines." A virtues correction along the lines of, "I need you to display (2) diligence and responsibility and (3) have your portion done by the end of the week" may be given if the employee kept missing deadlines.

Speaking the Language of Virtues offers supportive and helpful criticism. For instance, a leader speaking the language of virtues would remark, "Nice work remaining gracious with the difficult customer," as opposed to, "Nice work dealing with the difficult customer." Speaking the Language of Virtues necessitates the expression of a particular virtue (courtesy) and a particular circumstance (dealing with a difficult customer). The Virtues Project paradigm contends that using the language of virtues promotes moral development by connecting virtues to action and enhancing one's ability to draw upon a particular virtue when necessary. The first and most important TPV strategy—the one on which the other four tactics are based—is speaking the language of virtues.

TVP Strategy 2: Identify Teachable Moments

TVP's second tactic is to spot teachable moments. An attitude toward life as a process in which each of us is a life-long student is embodied through recognizing teachable moments. Recognizing Teachable Moments places a strong emphasis on "turning stumbling blocks into stepping stones." What virtue do you need? is a question that TVP resources advise asking when faced with difficulties or barriers.

For instance, a worker might have committed a mistake at work that had serious negative consequences. When the leader and the employee met to discuss the incident, the leader would start by asking the employee, "What happened?" and giving them the opportunity to respond. The supervisor would next inquire as to what qualities the employee had neglected to exhibit in that circumstance or which virtues would have enabled them to act morally. The manager would inquire, "Which virtues did you demonstrate that helped you do the right thing?" after the employee offered suggestions. The next question was, "How can you address the issue using the virtues you've named?" Using Teachable Moments offers a technique to learn from failures in a way that fosters virtues and directs future conduct by emphasizing lessons learned and implicit virtues.

TVP Strategy 3: Establish Clear Boundaries

Setting Clear Boundaries is the third TVP tactic. According to TVP, restorative justice and clear, wholesome, virtues-based limits can foster secure psychological settings that promote growth. "Safe havens" are created by establishing clear boundaries based on the "virtues of peace, fairness, respect, caring, and kindness." Setting Clear Boundaries, according to TVP, fosters environments where virtue and achievement are equally valued, where reparation is preferred versus retaliation, and where character development is made easier.

By outlining virtue-based standards, setting Clear Boundaries directs behavior. For instance, a leader may emphasize excellence as a desire rather than delivering a direction to produce better work. According to TVP, clear boundaries are easily understood, non-negotiable, moderate in number, explicit, focused on encouraged behavior rather than forbidden behavior, consistent and clearly articulated, and have appropriate, restorative consequences.

TVP Strategy 4: Uphold Spirit

Honoring Spirit is TVP's fourth tactic. "Spiritual" is defined by TVP as "a sense of meaning and purpose, beliefs and values, and mastery of the virtues in our character." In order to improve one's emotional and spiritual wellbeing, honoring Spirit entails setting aside time for introspection, awe, and appreciation of beauty. Honoring the spirit implies that life and living are about more than only meeting one's physical requirements and obtaining external benefits. Connecting with oneself, others, and the larger world is honoring the spirit. Nature walks, celebrations, ceremonies, meditation, mindfulness, prayer, introspection, honoring others, meditating on the wisdom of our elders, and reflecting on one's own qualities are all suggested activities for honoring spirit.

TVP Strategy 5: Offer Companionship

Offer Companioning is TVP's fifth tactic. Providing a way to fulfil the urge for people to "feel heard and recognized." A tactic used when someone is experiencing severe negative emotions, confusion, or a moral quandary is companioning. The following seven steps make up the prescribed compassionate curiosity of the companioning process:

1. When the door is opened, inquire "what's going on" or "what's going on for you?"

2. Provide attentive silence.

3. Specify the worst or hardest portion by asking these questions.

4. Pay attention to the senses.

5. Pose contemplation questions based on virtues, such as "what would give you the courage to... ", "how can you demonstrate... resolve," or "what would help you be patient in..."

6. Ask questions to help with integration, such as "Has this been useful?" or "What is clearer to you now?"

7. Express admiration for a virtue: "I have really heard your compassion in wishing to..." or "I love the loyalty you have demonstrated for..."

The foundation of companioning is the idea that we already possess the wisdom needed to deal with problems, losses, and disappointments rather than needing to get it from someone else. This is in line with counselling and coaching methods that focus on assisting the speaker in discovering his or her personal ideal course of action.

Additional Ideas for Including Virtues in Leadership Development

In his research of ethical leadership, J.B. Brown makes the case that creating virtuous leaders begins with identifying, shaping, and building one's own basic principles through time. His analysis is conclusive on this. Over 95% of the 3,257 executives and workers who established their core values through facilitation and coaching from 2002 to 2009 chose integrity as the most significant virtue. Behavioral indicators including honesty, truth, ethics, justice, and doing the right thing were among the most constant, despite modest variations in how they characterized it. When contrasted to their current conduct, many people found that developing their personal core principles and increasing their ethical awareness had a profound impact on their lives.

Before anyone rushes out and decides to start the process of creating morally upright leaders within their firm, remember that there is a serious warning to heed, advises Brown. People are virtually always drawn to and wish to imitate virtuous ethical leadership when they first begin to examine what that looks like. Unintentionally, this understanding causes individuals to quickly learn what immoral, self-centered leadership looks like and to despise it. Followers, especially those with awareness of what constitutes a virtuous and ethical leader, disengage and/or depart in disgust when executives and managers talk the talk but don't walk the walk.

Brown suggests the following as components of virtuous leadership development:

1. Create an organization-wide shared vision, mission, and values. This sets the bar for behavior for all organization stakeholders and directs the organization in the direction that its leadership wants it to go. Applying an understanding of applied ethics, use a facilitation/coaching method to help the CEO and a small senior team:

   - What are ethics and making ethical decisions?

   - Why practice ethics? - benefits and difficulties

   - Discussion about a variety of justifications and rationalizations for unethical activity.

2. Create a prescriptive procedure for making ethical decisions that takes into account: The advantages and disadvantages of consequentialist, deontological, and virtuous/integrity applications (most people tend to filter right decisions from one of these applications). The trick is to be able to weigh the benefits and drawbacks of each and decide which application is most appropriate in a specific circumstance (ethics is grey, not black and white).

3. Create a decision-making matrix with ethical filters that will help you use consequentialist, deontological, and virtuous/integrity applications to help you come to the best conclusion.

4. Create corporate core values that include morality, not just organizational purposes.

5. Create a compliance structure that includes whistleblower protections for unethical, immoral, and values-violating activity.

6. Create a method to help each employee in the organization discover and communicate their personal value system.

7. Include moral and virtue-based conduct components in performance evaluation systems.

In his latest book, *Intentional Integrity: How Smart Companies Can Lead an Ethical Revolution,* Robert Chesnut, Chief Ethics Officer of Airbnb Inc., suggests six C's to promote corporate integrity:

- Chief Executive Officer is the first C since everything begins at the top. Any attempt at maintaining integrity will almost likely fail if the organization lacks a noble mission that the leadership is dedicated to upholding.

- A Customized Code of Ethics is the second C. You need something particular and appropriate for your business; you cannot simply adopt someone else's code of ethics and call it your own.

- The third C stands for communicating the code, as staff members want to know that their new employer shares their beliefs.

- Having a clear reporting system is the fourth C. Employees must be made aware that when issues develop, you genuinely want to hear about them, and you need a framework that encourages open communication.

- Consequences is the fifth C. Leaders must demonstrate their commitment to enforcing policies even when a senior-level employee disobeys them.

- Constant is the sixth C. To create an environment where everyone may feed their inner good wolf, it is essential to have an open line of communication on the value of integrity.

Coaching for Character Strengths and Virtues

According to recent research, mainstream executive coaching programs focus on and emphasize the following areas:

- Developing a strong vision.
- Goal setting.
- Performance management.
- Change management.
- Developing resilience persistence.
- Stress management.
- Improving communication and interpersonal skills.
- Developing effective networks and relationships.
- Addressing difficult conversations and conflict management.
- Developing inspirational skills.
- Developing confidence.

- Managing teams.

But very few executive coaching programs focus extensively on the inner work of leaders — emotional intelligence, self-awareness and character development. Making these the core of leadership coaching would have a significant impact on improving the quality of leaders that are chosen and promoted.

Teaching Virtues Through Stories

In their chapter of the book *Research in Ethical Issues in Organizations*, Katalin Illes and Howard Harris make the case that "Stories can be employed in the development of organizational ethics." *To Kill a Mockingbird, 12 Angry Men, and Ulysses* are a few examples. They continue, "Case studies with obvious right/wrong answers and ethical challenges presented in narrative form engage individuals primarily on a rational level. They might increase someone's awareness of moral difficulties, but this relatively impersonal and detached awareness by itself won't compel that individual to behave morally.

Longer stories and those with developing characters might heighten peoples' emotional awareness and aid in bringing their subliminally held moral principles and ethical standards to the fore. Through the several plots that readers can follow from early childhood throughout their lives, they offer a more intimate experience where participants are emotionally invested and have a profound grasp of actions and their effects.

The study of fictional works where concerns of virtues and ethics are demonstrated could be a part of a robust leadership development program targeted at character development.

Developing Character-Based Leadership Through Guided Self-Reflection

As I outline in my book, *I Know Myself and Neither Do You*, self-awareness is one of the cornerstones to Emotional Intelligence, a key for good leadership. One method to achieve this is through self-reflection. Christa Kierscho and Nicole Gullekson, writing in *The International Journal of Management Education* propose a process for guided self-reflection for leaders (and potential leaders). They describe "a series of exercises according to experiential learning theory occurs in a dialectic, cyclical process involving concrete experiences, reflective observation, abstract conceptualization and active experimentation.

Developing Virtuous Leaders of Good Character: Principles to Follow

- Stress the importance of integrity in actions; demand it of ourselves, those we work with, and those who guide us.

- Stop appointing sociopathic/psychopathic, egotistical, and overconfident leaders to positions of authority in our institutions and organizations. Instead, choose leaders who are sincere, modest, and caring.

- Promote and hire more women into positions of leadership. According to research, female leaders are less likely to engage in dishonest or unethical activities.

- Undertake a thorough overhaul of the current capitalistic system, whose rules and procedures encourage immoral and unethical conduct as well as poor choices that harm people and the environment. Particularly, it is necessary to give up using shareholder interests as the main factor in corporate decisions.

- Promote increased support for the humanities in post-secondary education rather than the existing emphasis on technical knowledge and competence in business. Encourage business schools to place more emphasis on the study of humanities, especially philosophy and ethics.

- Motivate business executives (and their staff) to get more involved in deserving, non-profit endeavors that advance society and the environment.

- Strengthen laws, rules, policies, and procedures to protect anyone who come into contact with unethical (or immoral) corporate behaviors or who witness them.

- Stress the value of fostering emotional intelligence and self-awareness in leadership development programs and training.

- Promote leadership behaviors that increase exposure to different facets of racial, ethnic, and cultural (as well as gender) diversity.

- Encourage the public education system to incorporate the teaching of civics, moral and ethical behavior, critical thinking, and Socratic conversation into both teacher preparation and curriculum.

- Promote curriculum initiatives and hands-on learning opportunities for children in the public school system that promote social justice and environmental protection.

- Have "nice dialogues" with others about moral principles and decency.

- Collaborate with others to address important issues or challenges that affect everyone's well-being.

- Volunteer your time to a cause or initiative that helps people, the human race, or the environment without expecting credit or payment.

- Participate actively in the obligations of being a citizen in a democracy.

Final Thoughts and Questions to Consider

In some ways leadership development both in academic and organizational settings hasn't changed in decades, with a focus on themes such as planning, execution, vision and inspiration.

Questions to Consider

1. Why is it so difficult for leadership development initiatives to focus on good character and virtuous behavior?

2. If you were in charge of the leadership development program in your organization, where would you start to make the change?

Afterword

Writing *Virtuous Leadership* was in many ways for me, inspirational and uplifting. There is so much chaos and turmoil in the world right now, particularly in the U.S., where corrupt, unethical and amoral leaders of bad character are far too prevalent, causing great harm to the well-being of others and society as a whole.

It's not as though we don't know what kind of leaders are best for us—ethical, moral leaders of the highest character. We do. But we continue to hire the narcissists, self-serving leaders to do anything for personal gain or that of their tribe.

Both John Henry Newman in his *Idea of a University*, as well as Russell Kirk, in an essay entitled "Can Virtue Be Taught?" argue that we can teach people to be more virtuous. Newman argues "while a liberal education may very well provide one with the knowledge and discipline that makes virtue possible." Kirk argues "But it's also clear that there's little hope for America if the social order depends on a virtuous citizenry, but families aren't teaching virtue and schools can't do it."

Fortunately, we don't have to reinvent the wheel. We have at our disposal ancient philosophy, current research and plentiful examples of virtuous leadership and character. What remains is only our courage to take action upon this knowledge, first with families, then schools and then our organizations and institutions.

A failure to do so will be at our collective peril.

References

Adair, J. (2005). *How to Grow Leaders. The Seven Key Principles of Effective Leadership Development*. Great Britain: Kogan Page Limited.

Adair, J. (2003). *Not Bosses but Leaders. The Way to Success*. Great Britain: Kogan Page Limited.

Alzola, M. (2008). Character and environment: The status of virtues in organizations. *Journal of Business Ethics, 3,* 343–357.

Alzo la, M. (2012). The possibility of virtue. *Business Ethics Quarterly, 22*(2), 377–404.

Anderson, G.L. (1997). Identity and character development: Individual in community. *International Journal of World Peace, 14*(4), 41-54.

Annas, J. (2012). Being virtuous and doing the right thing. In R. Shafer-Landau (Ed.), *Ethical theory: An Anthology* (2nd ed.). New York: Wiley.

Annas, J. (2015). Applying virtue to ethics (Society of Applied Philosophy Annual Lecture 2014). *Journal of Applied Psychology, 32*(1), 1–14.

Aquino, K., & Reed, A. (2002). The self-importance of moral identity. *Journal of Personality and Social Psychology, 83*(6), 1423–1440.

Aristotle. (350BCE/1962). *Nicomachean Ethics* (M. Ostwald, Trans.). Englewood Cliffs, New Jersey: Prentice Hall.

Arjoon, S. (2000). Virtue theory as a dynamic theory of business. *Journal of Business Ethics, 2,* 159–178.

Arjoon, S. (2008). Reconciling situational social psychology with virtue ethics. *International Journal of Management Reviews, 10*(3),221–243.

Ashar, H., & Lane-Maher, M. (2004). Success and spirituality in the new business paradigm. *Journal of Management Inquiry, 13*(3), 249–260.

Atkinson, T. N., & Butler, J. W. (2012). From regulation to virtue: A critique of ethical formalism in research organizations. *Journal of Research Administration, 43*(1), 17–32.

Austin, D. (2005). *The effects of a strengths development intervention program upon the self-perceptions of students' academic abilities.* Azusa Pacific University, Azusa, Ca. Dissertation Abstracts International, 66(05A), 1631–1772. (UMI No. AAT3175080).

Avolio, B. J., & Gardner, W. L. (2005). Authentic leadership development: Getting to the root of positive forms of leadership. *The Leadership Quarterly, 16*(3), 315–338.

Avolio, B. J., & Hannah, S. T. (2008). Developmental readiness: Accelerating leader development. *Consulting Psychology Journal: Practice and Research, 60*(4), 331–347.

Avolio, B. J., Reichard, R. J., Hannah, S. T., Walumbwa, F. O., & Chan, A. (2009). A meta-analytic review of leadership impact research: Experimental and quasi-experimental studies. *The Leadership Quarterly, 20*(5), 764–784.

Axline, L. L. (1996). *Shared Values and ethics awareness—Hitting the targets*. San Antonio, TX: Holt Consulting Services, Inc.

Badarocco, J.L. (1997). *Defining Moments*. Boston, Massachusetts: Harvard Business School Press.

Bandura, A. (1976). *Social Learning Theory*. Englewood Cliffs, NJ: Prentice-Hall.

Bandura, A. (1997). *Self-Efficacy: The Exercise of Control*. New York, NY: Freeman.

Barclay, L. A., Markel, K. S., & Yugo, J. E. (2012). Virtue theory and organizations: Considering persons with disabilities. *Journal of Managerial Psychology*, 27(4), 330–346.

Barge, J. K. (2014). Pivotal leadership and the art of conversation. *Leadership, 10*(1), 56–78

Barger, R.N. (2000). *A summary of Lawrence Kohlberg's stages of moral development*. University of Notre Dame. Retrieved on August, 12, 2006.

Barker, R. A. (2002). An examination of organizational ethics. *Human Relations, 55*(9), 1097–1116.

Barnard, H. (2003). *The Anthropological Presuppositions of Personal and Professional Leadership*. Unpublished masters essay. Johannesburg: Rand Afrikaans University.

Barrick, M. R., & Mount, M. K. (1990). The big five personality dimensions and job performance: A meta-analysis. *Personnel Psychology*, 44(1), 1–26.

Bass, B. M., & Avolio, B. J. (1995). *The Multifactor Leadership Questionnaire.* Palo Alto: Mind Garden Inc.

Bass, B. M., & Riggio, R. E. (2006). *Transformational Leadership.* Mahwah, NJ: Lawrence Erlbaum Associates.

Bass, B. M., & Steidlmeier, P. (1999). Ethics, character, and authentic transformational leadership behavior. *Leadership Quarterly,* 10(2), 181–217.

Bass, B. M. (1985). *Leadership and Performance Beyond Expectations.* New York: Free Press.

Bass, B. M., & Avolio, B. J. (1995). *The Multifactor Leadership Questionnaire.* Palo Alto: Mind Garden Inc.

Bauman, D. (2017). The drive to virtue: A virtue ethics account of leadership motivation. In A. J. G. Sison, G. R. Beabout, & I. Ferrero (Eds.), *Handbook of Virtue Ethics in Business and Management* (pp. 961–971). Dordrecht: Springer.

Beatty, R., Ewing, J.R & Tharp, C. (2003). HR's role in corporate governance: present and prospective. *Human Resource Management,* 42(3), 3.

Bellingham, R. (2003). *Ethical leadership: Rebuilding Trust in Corporations.* Amherst, Mass: HRD Press.

Biswas-Diener, R., Kashdan, T. B., & Minhas, G. (2011). A dynamic approach to psychological strength development and intervention. *The Journal of Positive Psychology,* 6(2), 106–118.

Bragues, G. (2006). Seek the good life, not money: The Aristotelian approach to business ethics. *Journal of Business Ethics, 67*(4), 341–357.

Brebner, J., Donaldson, J., Kirby, N., & Ward, L. (1995). Relationships between happiness and personality. *Personality and Individual Differences, 19*(2), 251–258.

Bright, D. S., Alzola, M., Stansbury, J., & Stavros, J. M. (2011). Virtue ethics in positive organizational scholarship: An integrative perspective. *Canadian Journal of Administrative Sciences, 28*(3), 231–243.

Brown, M. E., & Trevi o, L. K. (2006). Ethical leadership: A review and future directions. *The Leadership Quarterly, 17*, 595–616.

Brown, J. B. (2011). The building of a virtuous transformational leader. *The Journal of Virtues & Leadership, 2*(1), 6–14.

Brown, M. E., & Trevin˜o, L. K. (2009). Leader-follower values congruence: Are socialized charismatic leaders better able to achieve it? *Journal of Applied Psychology, 94*(2), 478–490.

Brousselle, A., & Champagne, F. (2011). Program theory evaluation: Logic analysis. *Evaluation and Program Planning, 34*, 69–78.

Burke, R. J., Page, K. M., & Cooper, C. L. (Eds.). (2015). *Flourishing in Life, Work and Careers: Individual Wellbeing and Career Experiences.* Northampton: Edward Elgar Publishing.

Burns, J. M. (1978). *Leadership.* New York: Harper & Row.

Cameron, K. (2011). Responsible leadership as virtuous leadership. *Journal of Business Ethics, 98*, 25–35.

Cameron, K., & McNaughtan, J. (2014). Positive organizational change. *Journal of Applied Behavioral Science*, , 50(4), 445–462.

Cameron, K., Mora, C., Leutscher, T., & Calarco, M. (2011). Effects of positive practices on organizational effectiveness. *Journal of Applied Behavioral Science, 47*(3), 266–308.

Cameron, K., Quinn, R., & Dutton, J. (2003). *Positive Organizational Scholarship: Foundations of a New Discipline* (1st ed.). San Francisco: Berrett-Koehler.

Cavanagh, G. F., & Bandsuch, M. R. (2002). Virtue as a benchmark for spirituality in business. *Journal of Business Ethics, 38*(1/2), 109–117.

Ciulla, J. B. (2004a). Ethics and leadership effectiveness. In J. Antonakis, A. T. Cianciolo, & R. J.Sternberg (Eds.), *The Nature of Leadership* (pp. 302–327). Thousand Oaks, California: SAGE.

Ciulla, J. B. (2004b). "What is good leadership?" Working Papers Centre for Public Leadership, 116–122.

Ciulla, J. B. (Ed.). (2014). *Ethics, the Heart of Leadership* (3rd ed.). Santa Barbara: Praeger.

Ciulla, J. B. (2017). Leadership, virtue, and morality in the miniature. In A. J. G. Sison, G. R. Beabout, & I. Ferrero (Eds.), *Handbook of Virtue Ethics in Business and Management* (pp.941–949). Dordrecht: Springer.

Conger, J. A. (1991). Inspiring others: The language of leadership. *Academy of Management Perspectives, 5*(1), 31–45.

Crawford, J. A., & Kelder, J. (2019). Do we measure leadership effectively? Articulating and evaluating scale development psychometrics for best practice. *The Leadership Quarterly, 30*(1), 133–144.

Cropanzano, R., Bowen, D. E., & Gilliland, S. W. (2007). The management of organizational justice. *Academy of Management Perspectives, 21*(4), 34–48.

Crossan, M. M., Byrne, A., Seijts, G. H., Reno, M., Monzani, L., & Gandz, J. (2017). Toward a framework of leader character in organizations. *Journal of Management Studies, 54*(7), 986–1018.

Crossan, M., Lane, H. W., & White, R. E. (1999). An organizational learning framework: From intuition to institution. *Academy of Management Review, 24*(3), 522–537.

Crossan, M., Mazutis, D., Seijts, G., & Gandz, J. (2013). Developing leadership character in business programs. *Academy of Management Learning&Education,12*(2),285-305.

Crossan, M., Byrne, A., Seijts, G., Reno, M., Monzani, L., & Gandz, J. (2017). Toward a framework of leader character in organizations. *Journal of Management Studies, 54*(7), 986 — 1018.

Crossan, M., Seijts, G., & Gandz, J. (2016). *Developing Leadership Character*. New York, NY: Routledge Publishing.

Catalano, R., Berglund, M., Ryan, J., Lonczak, H., & Hawkins, J. (2004). Positive youth development in the United States: Research findings on evaluations of positive youth development programs. *The Annals of the American Academy of Political and Social Science, 591*(1), 98.

Clifton, D., & Harter, J. (2003). Investing in strengths. In A. K. S. Cameron, J. E. Dutton, & C. R. E. Quinn (Eds.), *Positive Organizational Scholarship: Foundations of a New Discipline*. San Francisco: Berrett-Koehler Publishers, Inc.

Cohen, J. (1988). *Statistical power analysis for the behavioral sciences*. UK: Lawrence Erlbaum.

Cox, K. (2006). Investigating the impact of strength-based assessment on youth with emotional or behavioral disorders. *Journal of Child and Family Studies, 15*(3), 278–292.

Caldwell, C., Dixon, R. D., Floyd, L. A., Chaudoin, J., Post, J., & Cheokas, G. (2012).

Cameron, K. (2011). Responsible leadership as virtuous leadership. *Journal of Business Ethics*, 98(1), 25–35.

Cameron, K. S., Bright, D., & Caza, A. (2004). Exploring the relationships between organizational virtuousness and performance. *The American Behavioral Scientist*, 47(6), 766–790.

Cavanagh, G. E., & Bandsuch, M. R. (2002). Virtue as a benchmark for spirituality in business. *Journal of Business Ethics*, 38(1/2), 109–117.

Cawley, M. J., Martin, J. E., & Johnson, J. A. (2000). A virtues approach to personality. *Personality and Individual Differences*, 28(5), 997–1013.

Chan, J. (2003). Giving priority of the worst off: A Confucian perspective on social welfare. In D. A. Bell & H. Chaibong (Eds.), *Confucianism for the Modern World*. UK: Cambridge University Press.

Christie, R., & Geis, F. L. (1970). *Studies in Machiavellianism*. New York: Academic Press.

Chun, R. (2005). Ethical character and virtue of organizations: An empirical assessment and strategic implications. *Journal of Business Ethics*, 57(3), 269–284.

Ciulla, J. B. (2004). Ethics and leadership effectiveness. In J. Antonakis, A. T. Cianciolo, & R. J. Sternberg (Eds.), *The Nature of Leadership*. Thousand Oaks, CA: Sage.

Conger, J. A., & Kanungo, R. N. (1998). *Charismatic Leadership in Organizations*. Thousand Oaks, CA: Sage.

Conway, J. M., & Lance, C. E. (2010). What reviewers should expect from author regarding common method bias in organizational research. *Journal of Business Psychology,* 25(3), 325–334.

Crossan, M., Mazutis, D., & Seijts, G. (2013). In search of virtue: The role of virtues, values, and character strengths in ethical decision making. *Journal of Business Ethics*, 113(4), 567–581.

Collins, J. C. (2001). Good to Great: Why Some Companies Make the Leap — and Others Don't (1st ed.). New York, NY: Harper Business.

Cashman, K. (1998). *Leadership from the Inside-Out*. Provo: Executive Excellence Publishing.

Covey, S.R. (1997). Seven habits of global executives. *Executive Excellence, 14* (12), 3-4.

Covey, S.R. (2004). *The 8th Habit. From Effectiveness to Greatness.* Great Britain: Simon & Schuster.

Cresswell, J.W. (1998). *Qualitative Inquiry and Research Design: Choosing Among Five Traditions.* California: Sage Publications.

Day, D., Fleenor, J., Atwater, L., Sturm, R., & McKee, R. (2014). Advances in leader and leadership development: A review of 25 years of research and theory. *The Leadership Quarterly, 25,* 63–82.

Day, D., & Harrison, M. (2007). A multilevel, identity-based approach to leadership development. *Human Resource Management Review, 17,* 360–737.

Day, D., & Liu, Z. (2018). What is Wrong with leadership development and what might be done with it? In R. E. Riggio (Ed.), *What's Wrong with Leadership? Improving Leadership Theory, Research, and Practice. London: Routledge.*

Dinh, J. E., Lord, R. G., Gardner, W. L., Meuser, J. D., Liden, R. C., & Hu, J. (2014). Leadership theory and research in the new millennium: Current theoretical trends and changing perspectives. *The Leadership Quarterly, 25*(1), 36–62.

De Bruin, B. (2013). Epistemic virtues in business. *Journal of Business Ethics,* 113, 583–595.

Dyer, J., & Chu, W. (2003). The role of trustworthiness in reducing transaction costs and improving performance: Empirical evidence from the United States, Japan, and Korea. *Organization Science,* 14(1), 57–68.

Dawson, L. (2005). Philosophy, work ethic and business ethics (Reflections from Hegel and Nietzsche). *The Journal of Corporate Citizenship*, 19(1), 55–64.

Day, D. V., & Antonakis, J. (2012). *The Nature of Leadership*. Thousand Oaks, CA: Sage.

DeNeve, K., & Cooper, H. (1998). The happy personality: A metanalysis of 137 personality traits and subjective well-being. *Psychological Bulletin*, 124(2), 197–229.

Derue, D. S., Nahrgang, J. D., Wellman, N., & Humphrey, S. E. (2011). Trait and behavioral theories of leadership: An integration and meta-analytic test of their relative validity. *Personnel Psychology*, 64(1), 7–52.

Diddams, M., & Chang, G. C. (2012). Only human: Exploring the nature of weakness in authentic leadership. *The Leadership Quarterly*, 23(3), 593–603.

Diener, E., Suh, E. M., Lucas, R. E., & Smith, H. L. (1999). Subjective well-being: Three decades of progress. *Psychological Bulletin*, 125(2), 276–302.

Dirks, K. T., & Ferrin, D. L. (2002). Trust in leadership: Metanalytic findings and implications for research and practice. *Journal of Applied Psychology*, 87(4), 611–628.

Dyck, B., & Kleysen, R. (2001). Aristotle's virtues and management thought: An empirical exploration of an integrative pedagogy. *Business Ethics Quarterly*, 11(4), 561–574.

Johnson, C. E. (2009). *Meeting the Ethical Challenges of Leadership: Casting Light or Shadow* (3rd ed.). Los Angeles: SAGE.

Deci, E., & Ryan, R. (2000). The "what" and "why" of goal pursuits: Human needs and the self-determination of behavior. *Psychological Inquiry, 11*(4), 227–268.

Diener, E., Emmons, R. A., Larsen, R. J., & Griffin, S. (1985). The satisfaction with life scale. *Journal of Personality Assessment, 49*(1), 71–75.

Diener, E., Lucas, R. E., & Scollon, C. N. (2006). Beyond the hedonic treadmill: Revising the adaptation theory of well-being. *American Psychologist, 61*(4), 305.

Dweck, C. (1986). Motivational processes affecting learning. *American Psychologist, 41*(10), 1040–1048.

Forster, J. (1991). Facilitating positive changes in self-constructions. *Journal of Constructivist Psychology, 4*(3), 281–292.

Edmondson, A. C., Kramer, R. M., & Cook, K. S. (2004). Psychological safety, trust, and learning in organizations: A group-level lens. In R. M. K. K. S. Cook (Ed.), *Trust and Distrust in Organizations: Dilemmas and Approaches* (Vol. 12, pp. 239–272). New York: SAGE.

Edmondson, A. C., & Lei, Z. K. (2014). Psychological safety: The history, renaissance, and future of an interpersonal construct. *Annual Review of Organizational Psychology and Organizational Behavior, 1,* 23–43

Emmons, R. A., & Diener, E. (1985). Personality correlates of subjective well-being. *Personality and Social Psychology Bulletin, 11*(1), 89–97.

Fehr, R., Kai Chi, Y. A. M., & Dang, C. (2015). Moralized leadership: The construction and consequences of ethical leadership perceptions. *Academy of Management Review, 40*(2), 182–209.

Fredrickson, B. L. (2001). The role of positive emotions in positive psychology—The broaden-and-build theory of positive emotions. *American Psychologist, 56*(3), 218–226.

Farmer, R.T. (2005). Corporate culture defines a company and future. *Mid-American Journal of Business, 20* (2), 7-9.

Fox Eades, J. (2008). *Celebrating strengths: Building Strengths-Based Schools.* Warwick, UK: CAPP Press.

Fredrickson, B. (1998). What good are positive emotions? *Review of General Psychology, 2*(3), 300–319.

Fredrickson, B., & Joiner, T. (2002). Positive emotions trigger upward spirals toward emotional well-being. *Psychological Science, 13*(2), 172–175.

Froh, J. J., Kashdan, T. B., Ozimkowski, K. M., & Miller, N. (2009). Who benefits the most from a gratitude intervention in children and adolescents? Examining positive affect as a moderator. *The Journal of Positive Psychology, 4*(5), 408–422.

Fairholm, M. R., & Fairholm, G. W. (2009). *Understanding Leadership Perspectives: Theoretical and Practical Approaches.* New York: Springer.

Fatt, J. P. T. (2000). Charismatic leadership. *Equal Opportunities International,* 19(8), 24–28.

Flynn, G. (2008). The virtuous manager: A vision for leadership in business. *Journal of Business Ethics, 78*(3), 359–372.

Fowers, B. J. (2008). From continence to virtue: Recovering goodness, character unity, and character types for positive psychology. Theory & Psychology, 18(5), 629–653.

Freeman, G. T. (2011). Spirituality and servant leadership: A conceptual model and research proposal. *Emerging Leadership Journeys, 4*(1), 120–140.

Fry, L. W. (2003). Toward a theory of spiritual leadership. *Leadership Quarterly, 14*(6), 693–727.

Fry, L. W., & Slocum, J. W. (2008). Maximizing the triple bottom line through spiritual leadership. *Organizational Dynamics, 37*(1), 86–96.

Galvin, B., Waldman, D., & Balthazard, P. (2010). Visionary communication qualities as mediators of the relationship between narcissism and attributions of leader charisma. *Personnel Psychology, 63*(3), 509–537.

Graeff, C. L. (1983). The situational leadership theory: A critical view. *Academy of Management Review, 8*(2), 285–291.

Graham, J., Haidt, J., Koleva, S., Motyl, M., Iyer, R., Wojcik, S. P., et al. (2013). Moral foundations theory: The pragmatic validity of moral pluralism. *Advances in Experimental Social Psychology, 47,* 55–130.

Graham, J., Iyer, R., Nosek, B. A., Haidt, J., Koleva, S., & Ditto, P. H. (2011). Mapping the moral domain. *Journal of Personality and Social Psychology, 2,* 366–385.

Grant, A. M., & Berry, J. (2011). The necessity of others is the mother of invention: Intrinsic and prosocial motivations, perspective taking, and creativity. *Academy of Management Journal, 54*(1), 73–96.

Gray, K.R. & Clark, G.W. (2002). Addressing corporate scandals through business education. *International Journal of World Peace, 19* (4), 43-62.

Gandz, J., Crossan, M., Seijts, G., & Stephenson, C. (2010). *Leadership on Trial: A Manifesto for Leadership Development*. London, ON: The Richard Ivey School of Business.

Gilley, A., Gilley, J. W., & McMillan, H. S. (2009). Organizational change: Motivation, communication, and leadership effectiveness. *Performance Improvement Quarterly, 21*(4), 75—94.

Gable, S., Reis, H., Impett, E., & Asher, E. (2004). What do you do when things go right? The intrapersonal and interpersonal benefits of sharing positive events. *Journal of Personality and Social Psychology, 87*(2), 228–245.

Gillham, J. (2011). *Teaching positive psychology to adolescents: 3 year follow-up.* Paper presented as part of the symposium Positive Psychology in Schools, presented at The 2nd World Congress on Positive Psychology, Philadelphia, July 23–26, 2011.

Govindji, R., & Linley, P. (2007). Strengths use, self-concordance and well-being: Implications for strengths coaching and coaching psychologists. *Coaching Psychology Review, 2*(2), 143-154.

Govindji, R., & Linley, P. (2008). *An evaluation of celebrating strengths* [Report prepared for North Lincolnshire Local Education Authority].

Greenleaf, R. K. (2002). *Servant Leadership: A Journey into the Nature of Legitimate Power and Greatness.* New York: Paulist Press.

Hackett, R. D., & Wang, G. (2012). Virtues and leadership. An integrating conceptual framework founded in Aristotelian and Confucian perspectives on virtues. *Management Decision,* 50(5), 868–899.

Hannah, S. T., & Avolio, B. J. (2011). Leader character, ethos, and virtue: Individual and collective considerations. *Leadership Quar terly,* 22(5), 989–994.

Hersey, P., & Blanchard, K. H. (2007). *Management of Organizational Behavior* (Vol. 9). Upper Saddle River: Prentice hall.

Heugens, P. P. M. A. R., Kaptein, M., & van Oosterhout, J. (2008). Contracts to communities: A processual model of organizational virtue. *Journal of Management Studies,* 45(1), 100–121.

Holt, R. (2006). Principals and practice: Rhetoric and the moral character of managers. *Human Relations,* 59(12), 1659–1680.

Hunter, J.D. (2000). *The Death of Character.* New York: BasicBooks.

Haste, H. , Markoulis, D. & Helkama, K. (1999). Morality, wisdom and life-span. Chapter 7. In Demetriou, A., Doise, W. & van Lieshout, C. (Eds.). *Life Span Developmental Psychology.* England: John Wiley & Sons Ltd.

Hart, K. E., & Sasso, T. (2011). Mapping the contours of contemporary positive psychology. *Canadian Psychology/Psychologie Canadienne, 52*(2), 82.

Huang, L., Stroul, B., Friedman, R., Mrazek, P., Friesen, B., Pires, S., et al. (2005). Transforming mental health care for children and their families. *American Psychologist, 60*(6), 615-630.

Huebner, E. S. (1991). Initial development of the student's life satisfaction scale. *School Psychology International, 12*(3), 231-242.

Hannah, S. T., & Avolio, B. J. (2010). Moral potency: Building the capacity for character-based leadership. *Consulting Psychology Journal: Practice and Research, 62*(4), 291–310.

Hannah, S. T., Lester, P. B., & Vogelgesang, G. R. (2005). Moral leadership: Explicating the moral component of authentic leadership. In W. L. Gardner, B. J. Avolio, & F. O. Walumbwa (Eds.*)*, *Authentic Leadership Theory and Practice: Origins, Effects and Development* (pp. 43–81). Greenwich, CT: JAI Press.

Hart, D. (2001). Administration and the ethics of virtue: In all things, choose first for good character and then for technical expertise. In T. L. Cooper (Ed.), *Handbook of Administrative Ethics.* New York: Marcel Dekker Inc.

Hartman, E. M. (1998). The role of character in business ethics. *Business Ethics Quarterly, 8*(3), 547–559.

Hinkin, T. R. (1998). A brief tutorial on the development of measures for use in survey questionnaires. *Organizational Research Methods,* 1(1), 104–121.

Hooijberg, R., Lane, N., & Diverse, A. (2010). Leader effectiveness and integrity: Wishful thinking? *International Journal of Organizational Analysis,* 18(1), 59–75.

House, R. J., Hanges, P. J., Javidan, M., Dorfman, P. W., & Gupta, V. (2004). *Culture, Leadership, and Organizations: The GLOBE Study of 62 Societies* (Vol. 1). Thousand Oaks, CA: Sage.

House, R. J., & Howell, J. M. (1992). Personality and charismatic leadership. *Leadership Quarterly,* 3(2), 81–108.

Howell, J. M., & Avolio, B. J. (1992). The ethics of charismatic leadership: Submission or liberation? *Academy of Management Executive,* 6(2), 43–54.

Huang, C. (1997). *The Analects of Confucius.* New York: Oxford University Press.

Ilies, R., Morgeson, F.P., & Nahrgang, J.D. (2005). Authentic leadership and eudaemonic well-being: Understanding leader-follower outcomes. *The Leadership Quarterly, 16* (3), 373–394.

IWG. (2006). *Personal Well-Being Index.* International Well-being group. Melbourne: Australian Centre on Quality of Life, Deakin University.

Irwin, T. (1999). *Nicomachean Ethics/Aristotle:* Translated with introduction, notes, and glossary. Indianapolis: Hackett Publishing Company.

Johnson, C. E. (2005). *Meeting the Ethical Challenges of Leadership: Casting light or shadow* (2nd ed.). Thousand Oaks, CA: Sage Publications.

Jaworski, J. & Senge, P. (1996). *Synchronicity: The Inner Path of Leadership*. USA: Berrett-Koehler Publishers Inc.

Johnson, C. E. (2009). *Meeting the Ethical Challenges of Leadership: Casting Light or Shadow*. Los Angeles, CA: Sage.

Juurikkala, O. (2012). Likeness to the divinity? Virtues and charismatic leadership. *Electronic Journal of Business Ethics and Organization Studies*, 17(2), 4–14.

Kilburg, R. R. (2012). *Virtuous leaders: Strategy, Character, and Influence in the 21st Century*. Washington: American Psychological Association.

Khurana, R. & Snook, S. (2004). Developing leaders of character. In Gandossy, R. & Sonnenfeld, J. (Eds.). *Leadership and Governance from the Inside Out*. New Jersey: John Wiley & Sons Inc.

Klann, G. (2003). Character Study: Strengthening the heart of good leadership. *Leadership in Action*. 23 (3), 3-7.

Kotter, J. P. (1996). *Leading Change*. Boston, MA: Harvard Business Review Press.

Kamins, M., & Dweck, C. (1999). Person versus process praise and criticism: Implications for contingent self-worth and coping. *Developmental Psychology, 35*(3), 835–847.

Kabat-Zinn, J. (2015). Mindfulness. *Mindfulness*, 6(6), 1481–1483.

Kilburg, R. R. (2012). *Virtuous leaders: Strategy, character, and Influence in the 21st Century.* Washington: American Psychological Association.

Kim, S., & Kim, H. (2009). Does cultural capital matter? Cultural divide and quality of life. *Social Indicators Research,* 93(2), 295–313.

Kish-Gephart, J. J., Harrison, D. A., & Trevino, L. K. (2010). Bad apples, bad cases, and bad barrels: Meta-analytic evidence about sources of unethical decisions at work. *Journal of Applied Psychology,* 95(1), 1–31.

Knights, D., & O'Leary, M. (2006). Leadership, ethics and responsibility to the other. *Journal of Business Ethics,* 67(2), 125–137.

Knippenberg, D. (2012). Leadership and identity. In D. V. Day & J.Antonakis (Eds.), *The Nature of Leadership* (pp. 477–507). Thousand Oaks, CA: Sage.

Kohlberg, L. (1976). Moral stages and moralization. In T. Lickona (Ed.), *Moral Development and Behavior: Theory, Research and Social issues.* New York: Holt, Rinehart and Winston.

Kok, G., & Chan, Y. (2008). The Relevance and value of Confucianism in contemporary business ethics. *Journal of Business Ethics,* 77(3), 347–360.

Kreps, T. A., & Monin, B. (2011). Doing well by doing good? Ambivalent moral framing in organizations. *Research in Organizational Behavior,* 31(1), 99–123.

Kouzes, J. M., & Posner, B. Z. (2007). *The Leadership Challenge* (4th ed.). San Francisco: Jossey-Bass.

Lang, L., Irby, B. J., & Brown, G. (2012). An emergent leadership model based on Confucian virtues and east asian leadership practices. *International Journal of Educational Leadership Preparation, 7*(2), 1–14.

Lara, F. J. (2012). The Oxford handbook of positive organizational scholarship. *Management Decision, 50*(3–4), 539–544.

Levine, M., & Boaks, J. (2014). What does ethics have to do with leadership? *Journal of Business Ethics, 124*(2), 225–242.

Luthans, F., & Youssef, C. M. (2007). Emerging positive organizational behavior. *Journal of Management, 33*, 321–349.

Luthans, F., Avey, J. B., Avolio, B. J., Norman, S. M., & Combs, G.M. (2006). Psychological capital development: Toward a micro-intervention. *Journal of Organizational Behavior, 27*, 387–393.

Lennick, D. & Kiel, F. (2005). *Moral Intelligence: Enhancing Business Performance and Leadership Success.* Upper Saddle River: Wharton School Publishers.

Lickona, T. (1991). *Educating for Character: How Our Schools Can Teach Respect and Responsibility.* New York: Bantam.

Latham, G., & Locke, E. (1991). Self-regulation through goal setting. *Organizational Behavior and Human Decision Processes, 50*(2), 212–247.

Linley, P. (2009). *Realise2: Technical Report.* Coventry, UK: CAPP Press.

Linley, P. A., & Harrington, S. (2006). Strengths coaching: A potential-guided approach to coaching psychology. *International Coaching Psychology Review, 1*(1), 37–46.

Linley, P. A., Maltby, J., Wood, A., Joseph, S., Harrington, S., Peterson, C.,… Seligman, M. E. P. (2007). Character strengths in the United Kingdom: The VIA inventory of strengths. *Personality and Individual Differences, 43*(2), 341–351.

Linley, P., Nielsen, K., Wood, A., Gillett, R., & Biswas-Diener, R. (2010). Using signature strengths in pursuit of goals: Effects on goal progress, need satisfaction, and well-being, and implications for coaching psychologists. *International Coaching Psychology Review, 5*(1), 8–17.

Linley, P. A., Woolston, L., & Biswas-Diener, R. (2009). Strengths coaching with leaders. *International Coaching Psychology Review, 4*(1), 37-46.

Locke, E., & Latham, G. (2002). Building a practically useful theory of goal setting and task motivation. *American Psychologist, 57*(9), 705–717.

Louis, M. C. (2008). *A comparative analysis of the effectiveness of strengths-based curricula in promoting first-year college student success.* Azusa Pacific University, Azusa, California. Dissertation Abstracts International, 69(06A). (UMI No. AAT 3321378).

Langer, E. J. (2014). *Mindfulness—25th Anniversary Edition.* Philadelphia, PA: Da Capo Press.

Lanctot, J. D., & Irving, J. A. (2010). Character and leadership: Situating servant leadership in a proposed virtues framework. *International Journal of Leadership Studies, 6*(1), 28–50.

Lau, D. C. (1979). *Confucius: The Analects.* Bungay: Richard Clay Ltd.

Li, C. (2009). Where does Confucian virtuous leadership stand? *Philosophy East and West*, 59(4), 531–536.

Lynch, P., Eisenberger, R., & Armeli, S. (1999). Perceived organizational support: Inferior versus superior performance by wary employees. *Journal of Applied Psychology*, 84(4), 467–483.

MacIntyre, A. (1985). *After Virtue: A Study in Moral Theory* (2nd ed. London: Duckworth.

MacIntyre, A. (1999). *Dependent Rational Animals: Why Human Beings Need the Virtues*. Peru: Open Court.

Manz, K. P., Marx, R. D., Neal, J. A., & Manz, C. C. (2006). The language of virtues: Toward an inclusive approach for integrating spirituality in management education. *Journal of Management, Spirituality & Religion*, 3(1/2), 104–125.

March, J. G. (1991). Exploration and exploitation in organizational learning. *Organization Science*, 2(1), 71–87.

Mayfield, J. R., Mayfield, M. P., & Kopf, J. (1998). The effects of leader motivating language on subordinate performance and satisfaction. *Human Resource Management*, 37(3/4), 235-250.

Manning, G. & Curtis. K. (1998). *The Art of Leadership*. New York: Mc Graw Hill.

Maxwell, J.C. (1998). *The 21 Irrefutable Laws of Leadership*. Nashville: Thomas Nelson Publishers.

Maxwell, J.C. (2002). The most important ingredient of leadership: Integrity. In Graves, S.R. & Addington, T.G. *Life @ Work on Leadership*. San Francisco: Jossey-Bass.

McElmeel, S.L. (2002). *Character Education. A Guide Book for Teachers, Librarians and Parents*. USA: Libraries Limited.

Miller, G. (2004). Leadership and integrity: How to ensure it exists in your organization. *The Canadian Manager, 29* (4), 15-17.

Miller, J (2003) Organizational future solutions: Integrity. *Futurics, 27* (3/4), 105-106.

Martinez, A. C. (2001). *The Hard Road to the Softer Side: Lessons from the Transformation of Sears*. New York, NY: Crown Business.

Minhas, G. (2010). Developing realized and unrealized strengths: Implications for engagement, self-esteem, life satisfaction and well-being. *Assessment and Development Matters, 2*, 12–16.

Mitchell, J., Stanimirovic, R., Klein, B., & Vella-Brodrick, D. (2009). A randomized controlled trial of a self-guided internet intervention promoting well-being. *Computers in Human Behavior, 25*(3), 749–760.

Manz, C. C., Anand, V., Joshi, M., & Manz, K. P. (2008). Emerging paradoxes in executive leadership: A theoretical interpretation of the tensions between corruption and virtuous values. *The Leadership Quarterly*, 19(3), 385–392.

Mele, D. (2005). Ethical education in accounting: Integrating rules, values and virtues. *Journal of Business Ethics*, 57(1), 97–109.

Messick, D. (2006). Ethical judgment and moral leadership. In D. L. Rhode (Ed.), *Moral leadership: The Theory and Practice of Power, Judgment and Policy.* Hoboken: Wiley.

Narvaez, D. (2008). Human flourishing and moral development: Cognitive and neurobiological perspectives of virtue development. In L. Nucci & D. Narvaez (Eds.), *Handbook of Moral and*

Character Education. Mahwah NJ: Erlbaum.

Newstead, T., Macklin, R., Dawkins, S., & Martin, A. (2018). What is virtue? Advancing the conceptualization of virtue to inform positive organizational inquiry. *Academy of Management Perspectives, 32*(4), 443–457.

Nielsen, K., & Abildgaard, J. S. (2013). Organizational interventions: A research-based framework for the evaluation of both process and effects. *Work and Stress, 27*(3), 278–297.

Nielsen, K., & Miraglia, M. (2017). What works for whom in which circumstances? On the need to move beyond the 'what works?' question in organizational intervention research. *Human Relations, 70*(1), 40–62.

Nel, P.S., Gerber, P.D., van Dyk, P.S., Haasbroek, G.D., Schultz, H.B., Sono, T. & Werner, A. (2001). *Human Resource Management.* (5th ed.). Cape Town: Oxford University Press Southern Africa.

Newstrom, J.W. & Davis, K. (2002). *Organizational Behavior. Human Behavior at Work.* (11 ed.). United States: McGraw- Hill Companies, Inc.

Noe, R. (2005). *Employee Training and Development*. (3rd ed.). Boston: McGraw – Hill International.

Nucci, L. (1997). Moral development and character formation. In Walberg, H.J. & Haertel, G.D. *Psychology & Educational Practice*. Berkeley: MacCarchan.

Neubert, M. J. (2011). Introduction: The value of virtue to management and organizational theory and practice. *Canadian Journal of Administrative Sciences, 28*(3), 227–230.

Neubert, M., Carlson, D., Kacmar, K., Roberts, J., & Chonko, L. (2009). The virtuous influence of ethical leadership behavior: Evidence from the field. *Journal of Business Ethics, 90*(2), 157–170.

Okimoto, T. G., & Wenzel, M. (2014). Bridging diverging perspectives and repairing damaged relationships in the aftermath of workplace transgressions. *Business Ethics Quarterly, 24*(3), 443–473.

Oldenkamp, R., von Zelm, R., & Huijbregts, M. A. J. (2016, May). Valuing the human health damage caused by the fraud of Volkswagen. *Environmental Pollution, 212*, 121–127.

Pearce, C. L., Waldman, D. A., & Csikszentmihaly, M. (2006). Virtuous leadership: A theoretical model and research agenda. *Journal of Management, Spirituality & Religion, 3*(1/2), 60–77.

Peterson, C., & Seligman, M. E. P. (2004). *Character Strengths and Virtues: A Handbook and Classification*. Washington: American Psychological Association.

Popov, L. K., & Smith, K. (2005). *The Virtues Project Educator's Guide: Simple Ways to Create a Culture of Character*. Toronto: Ontario College of Teachers.

Park, N. (2004). Character strengths and positive youth development. In Peterson, C. Positive Development: Realizing the potential of youth. *The Annals of the American Academy of Political and Social Science* (Eds.). CA: Sage Publications.

Peterson, C. & Seligman, M.E.P. (2004). *Character Strengths and Virtues. A Handbook of Classification. American Psychological Association.* Oxford University Press.

Peterson, D. (2004). Perceived leader integrity and ethical intentions of subordinates. *Leadership & Organization Development Journal, 25* (1/2), 7-23.

Page, K., & Vella-Brodrick, D. (2010). *Working for wellness: Practical and creative methods for enhancing employee well-being.* Paper presented at The 2nd Australian Positive Psychology and Well-being Conference, Melbourne, 12–13 February, 2010.

Park, N. (2004). Character strengths and positive youth development. *The Annals of the American Academy of Political and Social Science, 591* (Positive Development: Realizing the Potential of Youth (Jan., 2004)), 25–39.

Park, N., & Peterson, C. (2006a). Moral competence and character strengths among adolescents: The development and validation of the Values in Action Inventory of Strengths for Youth. *Journal of Adolescence, 29*(6), 891–909.

Park, N., & Peterson, C. (2006b). Character strengths and happiness among young children: Content analysis of parental descriptions. *Journal of Happiness Studies, 7*(3), 323–341.

Park, N., & Peterson, C. (2008). Positive psychology and character strengths: Application to strengths-based school counseling. *Professional School Counseling, 12*(2), 85–92.

Popov, L. K. (2000). *The Virtues Project: Simple Ways to Create a Culture of Character: Educator's guide.* Los Angeles: Jalmar Press.

Prochaska, J., & Velicer, W. (1997). Behavior change: The transtheoretical model of health behavior change. *American Journal of Health Promotion, 12*(1), 38–48.

Proctor, C., Maltby, J., & Linley, P. A. (2011a). Strengths use as a predictor of well-being and health-related quality of life. *Journal of Happiness Studies, 12*(1), 153–169.

Proctor, C., Tsukayama, E., Wood, A. M., Maltby, J., Eades, J. F., & Linley, P. A. (2011). Strengths gym: The impact of a character strengths-based intervention on the life satisfaction and well-being of adolescents. *The Journal of Positive Psychology, 6*(5), 377–388.

Pless, N. M. (2007). Understanding responsible leadership: Roles identity and motivational drivers. *Journal of Business Ethics, 74*(4), 437–456.

Pless, N. M., & Maak, T. (2011). Responsible leadership: Pathways to the future. *Journal of Business Ethics, 98*(1), 3–13.

Popov, L., Popov, D., Kavelin, J. H., et al. (2006). Virtues reflection cards—A set of 100 contemplative cards. *The Virtues Project International*.

Page, K. M., & Vella-Brodrick, D. A. (2009). The 'what', 'why' and 'how' of employee well-being: A new model. *Social Indicators Research*, 90(3), 441–458.

Palanski, M. E., & Vogelgesang, G. R. (2011). Virtuous creativity: The effects of leader behavioral integrity on follower creative thinking and risk taking. *Canadian Journal of Administrative Sciences*, 28(3), 259–269.

Palanski, M. E., & Yammarino, F. J. (2007). Integrity and leadership: Clearing the conceptual confusion. *European Management Journal*, 25(3), 171–184.

Palanski, M. E., & Yammarino, F. J. (2009). Integrity and leadership: A multi-level conceptual framework. *Leadership Quarterly*, 20(3), 405–420.

Pearce, C. L. (2007). The future of leadership development: The importance of identity, multi-level approaches, self-leadership, physical fitness, shared leadership, networking, creativity, emotions, spirituality and on-boarding processes. *Human Resource Management Review*, 17, 355–359.

Pearce, C. L., Waldman, D. A., & Csikszentmihalyi, M. (2006). Virtuous leadership: An agenda for personal excellence. *Journal of Management, Spirituality & Religion*, 3(1/2), 60–77.

Prottas, D. J. (2013). Relationships among employee perception of their manager's behavioral integrity, moral distress, and employee attitudes and well-being. *Journal of Business Ethics*, 113(1), 51–60.

Quesnell, D. (2001). *Values Based Leadership Participant Guide.* Training Material. San Antonio, TX: Holt Caterpiller.

Riggio, R. E., Zhu, W., Reina, C., & Maroosis, J. A. (2010). Virtue- based measurement of ethical leadership: The leadership virtues questionnaire. *Consulting Psychology Journal: Practice and Research, 62*(4), 235–250.

Rossouw, G.J. & van Vuuren, L.J. (2003). Modes of Managing Morality: A Descriptive Model of Strategies for Managing Ethics. *Journal of Business Ethics, 46* (4), 389-402.

Randolph, J., & Edmondson, R. (2005). Using the binomial effect size display (BESD) to present the magnitude of effect sizes to the evaluation audience. *Practical Assessment Research & Evaluation, 10*(14), 1–7.

Rashid, T. (2004). *Enhancing strengths through the teaching of positive psychology*. Dissertation Abstracts International, 64, 6339.

Rath, T. (2007). *Strengths Finder 2.0*. New York: Gallup Press.

Reis, H. T., Sheldon, K. M., Gable, S. L., Roscoe, J., & Ryan, R. M. (2000). Daily well-being: The role of autonomy, competence, and relatedness. *Personality and Social Psychology Bulletin, 26*(4), 419.

Reivich, K., Seligman, M., Gillham, J., Linkins, M., Peterson, C., Duckworth, A., et al. (2003). *Positive psychology program for high school students: Lessons for the pleasant life, the good life and the meaningful life.* Unpublished manuscript.

Rosenthal, R., & Rubin, D. B. (1982). A simple, general purpose display of magnitude of experimental effect. *Journal of Educational Psychology, 74*(2), 166-174.

Rust, T., Diessner, R., & Reade, L. (2009). Strengths only or strengths and relative weaknesses? A pre- liminary study. *The Journal of Psychology: Interdisciplinary and Applied, 143*(5), 465–476.

Ryan, R., & Deci, E. (2000). Self-determination theory and the facilitation of intrinsic motivation, social development, and well-being. *American Psychologist, 55*(1), 68–78.

Reave, L. (2005). Spiritual values and practices related to leadership effectiveness. *The Leadership Quarterly, 16*(5), 655–687.

Resick, C. J., Hanges, P. J., Dickson, M. W., & Mitchelson, J. K. (2006). A cross-cultural examination of the endorsement of ethical leadership. *Journal of Business Ethics, 63*(4), 345–359.

Rhode, D. L. (2006). *Moral Leadership: The Theory and Practice of Power, Judgement and Policy.* Hoboken N.J.: Wiley.

Riggio, R. E., Zhu, W., Reina, C., & Maroosis, J. A. (2010). Virtue-based measurement of ethical leadership: The leadership virtues questionnaire. *Consulting Psychology Journal: Practice and Research, 62*(4), 235–250.

Ruiz-Palomino, P., & Martinez-Canas, R. (2011). Supervisor role modeling, ethics-related organizational policies, and employee ethical intention: The moderating impact of moral ideology. *Journal of Business Ethics*, 102(4), 653–668.

Sarros, J. C., & Cooper, B. K. (2006). Building character: A leadership essential. *Journal of Business and Psychology, 21*(1), 1–22.

Solomon, R. C. (1993). *Ethics and Excellence: Cooperation and Integrity in Business*. New York: Oxford University Press.

Sankar, Y. (2003). Character not charisma is the critical measures of leadership excellence. *Journal of Leadership & Organizational Studies, 9* (4), 45-55.

Spears, L.C. (2006). On character and servant leadership: Ten characteristics of effective, caring leaders. *The Greenleaf Centre for Servant Leadership*.

Storr, L. (2004). Leading with integrity: A qualitative research study. *Journal of Health Organization and Management*, (18)6, 415-434.

Seijts, G. (2014). *Good Leaders Learn: Lessons from Lifetimes of Leadership*. New York, NY: Routledge Publishing.

Seijts, G., Crossan, M., & Carleton, E. (2017). Embedding leader character into HR practices to achieve sustained excellence. *Organizational Dynamics, 46*(1), 30—39.

Seijts, G., & Roberts, M. (2011). The impact of employee perceptions on change in a municipal government. *Leadership and Organization Development Journal, 32*(2), 190—213.

Sosik, J. J., Gentry, W. A., & Chun, J. U. (2012). The value of virtue in the upper echelons: A multisource examination of executive character strengths and performance. *LeadershipQuarterly, 23*(3), 367–382.

Seligman, M. (2002). *Authentic Happiness*. New York: Free Press.

Seligman, M., & Csikszentmihalyi, M. (2000). Positive psychology: An introduction. *American Psychologist, 55*(1), 5–14.

Seligman, M. E. P., Ernst, R. M., Gillham, J., Reivich, K., & Linkins, M. (2009). Positive education: Positive psychology and classroom interventions. *Oxford Review of Education, 35*(3), 293–311.

Seligman, M., Steen, T., Park, N., & Peterson, C. (2005). Positive psychology progress. *American Psychologist, 60*(5), 410–421.

Sheldon, K., & Elliot, A. (1999). Goal striving, need satisfaction, and longitudinal well-being: The self- concordance model. *Journal of Personality and Social Psychology, 76*, 482–497.

Sheldon, K., & Houser-Marko, L. (2001). Self-concordance, goal attainment, and the pursuit of happiness: Can there be an upward spiral? *Journal of Personality and Social Psychology, 80*(1), 152–165.

Sheldon, K., Ryan, R., & Reis, H. (1996). What makes for a good day? Competence and autonomy in the day and in the person. *Personality and Social Psychology Bulletin, 22*(12), 1270-1281.

Sin, N., & Lyubomirsky, S. (2009). Enhancing well-being and alleviating depressive symptoms with positive psychology interventions: A practice-friendly meta-analysis. *Journal of Clinical Psychology, 65*(5), 467–487.

Schüz, M. (2012). Sustainable corporate responsibility — The foundation of successful business in the new millennium: Central European Business. *Virtue Ethics, Corporate Identity and Success*

Review, 2, 7–15.

Schüz, M. (2017). Foundations of ethical corporate responsibility. Winterthur: ZHAW School of Management and Law (English translation of: Schüz,M. (2013).

Schüz, M. (2019). *Applied Business Ethics - Foundations for Study and Daily Practice*. Singapore, New Jersey, London: World Scientific (English translation)

Shapiro, S. L., Wang, M. C., & Peltason, E. H. (2015). What is mindfulness, and why should organizations care about it? In J. Reb & P. W. Atkins (Eds.), *Mindfulness in Organizations — Foundations, Research, and Applications* (pp. 256–284). Cambridge: Cambridge University Press.

Solomon, R. C. (1999). *A Better Way to Think About Business — How Personal Integrity Leads to Corporate Success*. Oxford and New York: Oxford University Press.

Sarros, J. C., Cooper, B. K., & Hartican, A. M. (2006). Leadership and character. *Leadership & Organization Development Journal*, 27(8), 682–699.

Seligman, M. E. P., & Csikszentmihalyi, M. (2000). Positive psychology: An introduction. *American Psychologist*, 55(1), 5–14.

Sendjaya, S., Sarros, J. C., & Santora, J. C. (2008). Defining and measuring servant leadership behavior in Organizations. *Journal of Management Studies*, 45(2), 402–424.

Shamir, B., House, R. J., & Arthur, M. B. (1993). The motivational aspects of charismatic leadership: A self-concept based theory. *Organization Science*, 4(4), 577–594.

Shanahan, K. J., & Hyman, M. R. (2003). The development of a virtue ethics scale. *Journal of Business Ethics*, 42(2), 197–208.

Shryack, J., Steger, M. F., Krueger, R. F., & Kallie, C. S. (2010). The structure of virtue: An empirical investigation of the dimensionality of the virtues in action inventory of strengths. *Personality and Individual Differences*, 48(6), 714–719.

Singer, M. (2000). Ethical and fair work behavior: A normative empirical dialogue concerning ethics and justice. *Journal of Business Ethics*, 28(3), 187–209.

Sison, A. J. G. (2003). *The Moral Capital of Leaders: Why Virtue Matters*. Cheltenham, UK: Edward Elgar.

Trevino, L. K., Hartman, L. P., & Brown, M. (2000). Moral person and moral manager: How executives develop a reputation for ethical leadership. *California Management Review*, 42(4), 128–142.

Taylor, C. C. W. (2006). *Aristotle: Nicomachean ethics* (Books II–IV). New York: Oxford University Press.

Thun, B., & Kelloway, E. K. (2011). Virtuous leaders: Assessing character strengths in the workplace. *Canadian Journal of Administrative Sciences, 28*(3), 270–283.

Wang, G., & Hackett, R. D. (2015). Conceptualization and measurement of virtuous leadership: Doing well by doing good. *Journal of Business Ethics, 137*, 1–25.

Weaver, G. R. (2017). Organizations and the development of virtue. In A. J. G. Sison, G. R. Beabout, & I. Ferrero (Eds.), *Handbook of Virtue Ethics in Business and Management* (pp. 613–621).Dordrecht: Springer.

Whetstone, J. T. (2001). How virtue fits within business ethics. *Journal of Business Ethics, 33*(2), 101–114.

Whetstone, J. T. (2017). Developing a virtuous organizational culture.In A. J. G. Sison, G. R. Beabout, & I. Ferrero (Eds.), *Handbook of Virtue Ethics in Business and Management* (pp. 623–633).Dordrecht: Springer.

Walton, C. (1988). *The Moral Manager.* New York: Harper & Row.

Weaver, G. (2006). Virtue in organizations: Moral identity as a foundation for moral agency. *Organization Studies, 27*(3), 341–368.

Whetstone, J. T. (2001). How virtue fits within business ethics. *Journal of Business Ethics, 33*(2), 101–114.

Whetstone, J. T. (2005). A framework for organizational virtue: The interrelationship of mission, culture and leadership. *Business Ethics: A European Review,* 14(4), 367–378.

Wright, T. A., & Goodstein, J. (2007). Character is not "dead" in management research: A review of individual character and organizational-level virtue. *Journal of Management,* 33(6),

928–958.

Wu, Y., & Tsai, P. J. (2012). Multidimensional relationships between paternalistic leadership and perceptions of organizational ethical climates. *Psychological Reports: Human Resources & Marketing,* 111(2), 509–52.

Appendix A

TVP List of Virtues and Their Definitions*

Acceptance: Embracing life on its own terms. Acceptance allows us to bend without breaking in the face of tests.

Accountability: The willingness to take full responsibility for our choices.

Appreciation: Seeing the good in life. Freely expressing gratitude.

Assertiveness: Telling the truth about what is just, setting clear boundaries.

Awe: Reverence and wonder, deep respect for the source of life.

Beauty: A sense of wonder and reverence for the harmony, color, and loveliness of the world. Calling on our creativity to add to the beauty in the world.

Caring: Giving tender attention to the people and things that matter to us. Listening with compassion, helping with kindness.

Certitude: An attitude of faith, confidence and certainty. Trusting that all will be well.

Charity: A giving heart, a generous way of viewing others and caring for their needs.

Cheerfulness: Seeing the bright side, looking for the good in whatever happens.

Cleanliness: Keeping our bodies, our thoughts and our spaces clean. An environment of order and beauty brings peace to our souls

Commitment: Caring deeply about a person, a goal or a belief. Willingness to give our all and keep our promises.

Compassion: Deep empathy for the suffering of others. Compassion flows freely from the heart when we let go of judgments and seek to understand.

Confidence: A sense of assurance that comes from having faith in ourselves and in life. Confidence allows us to trust that we have the strength to cope with whatever happens.

Consideration: Giving careful thought to the needs of others. Holding a decision in a contemplative and thoughtful way.

Contentment: The awareness of sufficiency, a sense that we have enough and we are enough. Appreciating the simple gifts of life.

Cooperation: Working together for a common goal, calling on the different gifts each of us has to offer.

Courage: Transforms fear into determination. Embracing life fully, without holding back, doing what must be done even when it is difficult or risky.

Courtesy: Treating others with kindness, tact and graciousness.

Creativity: The power of imagination. Being open to inspiration, which ignites our originality.

Decisiveness: Firmness of mind in taking a stand, reaching a conclusion, making a decision. It requires both courage and discernment.

Detachment: Experiencing our feelings without allowing them to control us. Stepping back and thoughtfully choosing how we will act rather than just reacting.

Determination: The power of intent that drives our dreams. Persevering until we meet our goals.

Devotion: Commitment to something we care about deeply. Wholehearted service to our life's purpose.

Dignity: Honoring the worth of all people, including ourselves and treating everyone with respect.

Diligence: Doing what needs to be done with care, concentration and single-pointed attention, giving our absolute best.

Discernment: Applying the wisdom of our intuition to discover what is essential and true, with contemplative vigilance. Clarity of the soul

Empathy: The ability to put ourselves in another's place, with compassion and understanding.

Endurance: Practicing perseverance and patience when obstacles arise hones our character and educates our souls. We welcome all that we are here to learn.

Enthusiasm: Being filled with spirit. Excitement about life and openness to the wonders each day holds. Acting wholeheartedly, with zeal and eagerness, holding nothing back.

Excellence: Giving our best to any task we do and any relationship we have.

Fairness: Seeking justice, giving each person their share, making sure that everyone's needs are met.

Faith: A relationship of trust. Belief in the reality of Grace.

Faithfulness: Loyalty to our beliefs, regardless of what happens. Being true to the people we love.

Fidelity: Abiding by an agreement, treating it as a sacred covenant. Complete faithfulness in our relationships.

Flexibility: The ability to adapt and change amid the fluctuating circumstances of life. Going with the flow.

Forbearance: Tolerating hardship with good grace. Not allowing the trials of life to steal our joy.

Forgiveness: Overlooking mistakes, and being willing to move forward with a clean slate. Forgiving others frees us from resentment. Forgiving ourselves is part of positive change.

Fortitude: Strength of character. The will to endure, no matter what happens, with courage and patience.

Friendliness: A spiritual essential. Reaching out to others with warmth and caring. The willingness to be an intimate companion.

Generosity: Giving fully, sharing freely. Trust that there is plenty for everyone.

Gentleness: Moving wisely, touching softly, speaking quietly and thinking kindly.

Grace: Openness to the bounties of life, trusting that we are held in God's love through all circumstances. Reflecting gentleness and beauty in the way we act, speak and move.

Gratitude: Freely expressing thankfulness and appreciation to others and for the gifts of life.

Helpfulness: Doing useful things that make a difference to others. Taking time for thoughtfulness.

Honesty: Being truthful, sincere, open, and genuine. The confidence to be ourselves.

Honor: Living with a sense of respect for what we know is right. Living up to the virtues of our character. Keeping our agreements with integrity.

Hope: Looking to the future with trust and faith. Optimism in the face of adversity.

Humanity: Having an attitude of caring and mercy to all people.

Humility: Being open to every lesson life brings, trusting that our mistakes are often our best teachers. Being thankful for our gifts instead of boastful.

Idealism: Caring about what is right and meaningful in life. Daring to have big dreams and then acting as if they are possible.

Independence: Self-reliance. Making our own choices confidently without undue influence from others. Perceiving the truth, with trust in our own discernment.

Initiative: Daring to be original. Using creativity to bring something new into the world.

Integrity: Standing on moral high ground. Keeping faith with our ideals and our agreements.

Joyfulness: An inner wellspring of peace and happiness. Enjoying the richness of life. Finding humor, even in the midst of hard times.

Justice: Being fair in all we do. Making amends when we have hurt or wronged others. Protecting everyone's rights, including our own.

Kindness: Showing compassion. Giving tender attention in ways that brings others happiness.

Love: The connection between one heart and another. Attraction, affection and caring for a person, a place, an idea, and for life itself.

Loyalty: Unwavering faithfulness and commitment to people and ideas we care about, through good times and bad.

Mercy: Blessing others with our compassion and forgiveness. Extending our tenderness beyond what is just or deserved.

Mindfulness: Living reflectively and meaningfully, with conscious awareness of our actions, our words and our thoughts.

Moderation: Being content with enough. Using self-discipline to create balance in our lives and to keep from overdoing. Healthy stewardship of our time and resources.

Modesty: Self-respect and quiet confidence. Accepting praise with humility and gratitude. A sense of respectful privacy about our bodies.

Nobility: Having high moral standards. Doing the right thing. Keeping faith with our true value as spiritual beings.

Obedience: Following what we know is right. Compliance with the law. Abiding by our deepest integrity and conquering our misplaced passions

Openness: Willingness to consider new ideas. Listening to others with humility and sincerity. Being receptive to the blessings and surprises of life.

Optimism: A positive, cheerful outlook. Nothing can destroy our hope.

Orderliness: Creating an environment of peace and order. Planning step by step instead of going in circles.

Patience: Waiting peacefully. Quiet hope and faith that things will turn out right.

Peacefulness: Inner calm and tranquility. Giving up the love of power for the power of love. Resolving conflict in a just and gentle way.

Perceptiveness: Clarity of insight. Understanding that is intuitive, discerning and accurate.

Perseverance: Staying the course for however long it takes. Steadfastness and persistence in pursuing our goals.

Prayerfulness: A relationship of faith and gratitude with a power and presence greater than ourselves. A conversation with God.

Purity: A process of freeing ourselves day by day from influences and attachments that keep us from being true to ourselves and to what we know is right.

Purposefulness: Awareness of the meaningfulness of our lives. Living by a clear vision and focusing our energy on the goal before us.

Reliability: Being dependable. Being a promise keeper. Taking responsibility with trustworthiness.

Resilience: The strength of spirit to recover from adversity. Overcoming obstacles by tapping into a deep well of faith and endurance.

Respect: An attitude of honoring oneself and others through our words and actions. Treating every person with dignity and courtesy.

Responsibility: The willingness to be accountable for our choices and also for our mistakes. Taking on what is ours to do with strength and reliability.

Reverence: An awareness of the sacredness of life. Living with wonder and faith. Having a routine of reflection.

Righteousness: Living by a code of spiritual rectitude. Impeccable integrity to what we know is right. Calling ourselves gently back when we go off track.

Sacrifice: The willingness to give up what is important to us for what we know is more important. Giving our all for our beliefs. Making our life a sacred offering.

Self-Discipline: The self-control to do only what we truly choose to do, without being blown off course by our desires. Establishing healthy and ennobling habits.

Serenity: Tranquility of spirit, with trust and faith that all will be well. Peacefulness in the midst of trials.

Service: Doing helpful things that make a difference to others. Investing excellence in everything we do. The contribution we make is the fruitage of our lives.

Simplicity: Content with the basic gifts of life, we let go of excess, clutter, and complexity. We savor the moment.

Sincerity: Being open and genuine. Our words and actions reflect a truthful heart.

Steadfastness: Being steady, persevering and dependable. Having the strength to remain true to our purpose in spite of obstacles that arise.

Strength: The inner power to withstand whatever comes. Endurance in the midst of tests.

Tact: Telling the truth kindly. Thinking before we speak, aware of how deeply our words affect others. Discerning what to say, when it is timely to say it, and what is better left unsaid.

Thankfulness: An attitude of gratitude for living, learning, loving and being. Generosity in expressing appreciation. Focusing on the blessings in our lives.

Thoughtfulness: Kindness and consideration guided by empathy brightens others lives. Being contemplative and discerning.

Tolerance: Being open to differences. Refraining from judgments. Patience and forgiveness with others and ourselves. Accepting things that we wish were different with humor and grace.

Trust: Having faith. Positive expectation that all will be well. Having confidence that the right thing will come about without trying to control it or make it happen. Being sure, in the depths of our being, that there is some gift or learning in everything that happens.

Trustworthiness: Being worthy of the trust others place in us. When we give our word, we stand by it. Keeping our agreements faithfully.

Truthfulness: Truth is the bedrock of integrity on which we build all our other virtues. An ongoing commitment to live by what is most real and authentic in our own nature. Honesty in all our dealings.

Understanding: Being insightful in our perceptions of ideas and feelings. Listening with compassion and accuracy to others' feelings.

Unity: Inclusiveness. Finding common ground in our diversity. Seeking peace in all circumstances.

Wisdom: Having a discerning mind, based on experience and mindfulness. Making wise decisions based on our deepest intuition.

Wonder: Being open to the beauty and mysteries of life. Our soul's appreciation for what is precious and inspiring.

Zeal: Fervent enthusiasm for what we believe to be important. Living by a strong sense of the value of life and faith.

Source: The Virtues Project (Kavelin-Popov, Dan Popov and John Kavelin, 1991).

Appendix B

Character in Decision-Making*

Dimensions of Leader Character	Decision-Making Description
Judgment	Based on pertinent information and a careful examination of the facts; makes wise conclusions quickly; recognises the bigger picture when making decisions. demonstrates adaptability when faced with novel facts or circumstances; possesses an understanding of how to move forward that is implicit; possesses a keen insight into complex problems. Effectively uses rationality in ambiguous situations.
Courage	Does the correct thing regardless if it's unpopular, deliberately discouraged, or could have a bad effect on them; demonstrates unwavering tenacity, assurance, and persistence when facing challenges.; swiftly bounces back after setbacks.

Drive	Strives for superiority. possesses an intense drive to succeed; demonstrates a sense of urgency in problem-solving; takes on obstacles with vigour and passion.
Collaboration	Promotes the creation and maintenance of harmonious interpersonal relationships; promotes open discussion and does not become defensive when questioned; possesses the capacity to relate to others on a deep level in a way that encourages the fruitful exchange of ideas; acknowledges that events can touch everyone regardless of where they occur.
Integrity	Holds oneself to a high moral standard and acts morally consistently, especially under trying circumstances; is viewed as acting in a way by others that is in line with their own personal values and views; adheres to the rules and guidelines of the organization
Temperance	Maintains a cool, collected demeanour; keeps their capacity to reason and act sensibly in stressful situations; completes tasks and finds solutions to issues in a meticulous, methodical manner; avoids excesses and maintains balance.

Accountability	Accepts responsibility for decisions and actions; is willing to take ownership of challenging issues.

Reliably delivers on expectations. Can becounted on in tough situations |
Justice	Makes an effort to guarantee that people are treated fairly and that contributions are rewarded or punished in proportion; maintains objectivity and limits personal prejudices when making decisions; gives people the chance to provide their thoughts on processes and procedures. gives prompt, detailed, and frank justifications for judgments. aims to make amends for wrongs both inside and beyond the organization.
Humility	Let your achievements do the talking. admits its limitations. recognises the value of carefully considering one's own beliefs and thoughts; accepts opportunities for one's own progress. does not believe that one is more significant or unique than others; respects other people; recognizes and values the contributions and abilities of others.
Humanity	Demonstrates genuine concern and care for others; is empathetic with others' values,

	feelings, and beliefs; can forgive and not hold grudges; understands that all people make mistakes and offers opportunities for individuals to learn from their mistakes.
Transcendence	Draws inspiration from accomplishments or a love of beauty in fields like sports, music, the arts, and design; identifies potential where others do not. has a broad perspective on things and considers both long-term and broad variables; shows a sense of direction in life.

Adapted from "Toward a framework of leader character" by Crossan et al. (2017).

Appendix C

Ethical Scenario Questions for Leaders to Assess Their Character and Virtues

Here are some ethical and character based questions that could be use for leadership training and evaluation purposes. The approach in the discussions should be answering the question, "what virtues or positive character traits" would need to be in evidence in your response?

1. What if your "good friend" causes trouble in the company, because he can't perform his job properly?

2. What would you do if a subordinate is constantly criticizing and challenging you in meetings?

3. What action would you take if a subordinate was making the same mistake repeatedly? What if it was your boss?

4. What would you do if you make a serious mistake but no-one sees you do it?

5. You are president of a local grassroots substance abuse prevention task force that has been organizing and supporting a wide spectrum of local substance abuse prevention activities during its five years of existence. You are currently staging a fund-raising campaign to raise money for scholarships to send 50 inner-city youth to prevention leadership camp. As the deadline for registration arrives, you have enough money for 21 scholarships, due primarily to severe economic cutbacks that have hit local businesses and industries in the past. A local

business, reading of this dilemma in the paper, approaches the task force and offers to donate the $3,900 to reach the goal of financing 50 youths' attendance to the camps. The local business offering this financial support is a beer brewery. What would you do?

6. A supplier sends a basket of expensive foodstuffs to your home at Christmas with a card: "We hope you and your family enjoy the 'goodies.'". What action(s) might you want to take?

7. You are in a head-to-head battle with your arch competitor. One of your co-workers approaches you. He has recently joined your company after having worked for a second competitor for several years. He suggests, "I made notes on all of other company's bids when I could get the data. They use some clear cost standards. Would you like me to bring my notes to the office tomorrow and let you look through them?" How do you respond?

8. You are the VP of a mid-size Tech company. The CFO of your company comes to you and tells you that the CEO has ordered the CFO to "cook the books" so that the Board of Directors don't realize the company is in financial difficulty. The CEO has a close relationship with the Chairman of the Board. What do you do?

Other Books by Ray Williams

Macho Men: How Toxic Masculinity Hurts Us All And What To Do About It

Toxic Bosses: Practical Wisdom for Developing Wise, Ethical and Moral Leaders

I Know Myself and Neither Do You: Why Charisma, Confidence and Pedigree Won't Take You Where You Want to Go

Eye of the Storm: How Mindful Leaders Can Transform Chaotic Workplaces

The Leadership Edge: Strategies to Transform School Systems

Dragon Tamer

Ready, Aim, Influence (contributing author)

Systemic Change: Touchstones for the Future School (contributing author)

About the Author

Ray Williams has provided executive coaching, speaking and professional consultations services worldwide. He has over 35 years' experience as a Superintendent of Schools, CEO, senior HR executive, management consultant, trainer, executive coach, hypnotherapist, professional speaker, and author. He has received his undergraduate and graduate training in History, English, Organizational Psychology and Leadership. He is a Certified Master Executive Coach and Certified Hypnotherapist.

He is currently retired as President and CEO of Ray Williams Associates, an executive coaching firm based in Vancouver, providing coaching and mentoring to executives in the public and private sectors worldwide. He also was an associate of ViRTUS Inc., a leadership development company based in Vancouver.

He is past president of the International Coach Federation in Vancouver and held several board positions professional associations in North America. In addition, he has served as a director and Vice-Chair for the Vancouver Board of Trade and director for several community organizations.

His clients have included Fortune 500 companies, the Best Managed Companies in Canada, and dozens of small businesses and entrepreneurial start-ups. He has been recognized as one of the top C-Suite coaches in Canada.

He has written extensively about leadership, the workplace, organizations, personal development, and social issues including two books on leadership; contributed to several books organizational issues; a novel and screenplay; and been interviewed or written articles for national publications and the media such as *The Financial Post, The Washington Post, Entrepreneur, The Globe and Mail,* the *Vancouver Sun, USA Today* and *Inc.,* and online media such as *Psychology Today, Fulfillment Daily, Business.com, Medium and Sivana East.*

Beyond his professional training and experience, he brings his insights into human behavior, having been born and raised in Hong Kong, where his family were imprisoned for four years by the Japanese in WWII, which allows him a unique perspective on overcoming adversity, and sustaining a positive outlook.

www.ingramcontent.com/pod-product-compliance
Lightning Source LLC
Chambersburg PA
CBHW071202210326
41597CB00016B/1649